D0263768

corporate governance

practical advice for directors
on today's most important
boardroom issue

managing editors:	Caroline Proud and Lesley Shutte
production manager:	Lisa Robertson
design:	Halo Design
commercial director:	Ed Hicks
publishing director:	Tom Nash
chief operating officer:	Andrew Main Wilson

Published for the Institute of Directors
and SAS by Director Publications Ltd
116 Pall Mall London SW1Y 5ED
Ⓣ 020 7766 8950 Ⓦ www.iod.com

© Copyright October 2004 Director Publications Ltd
A CIP record for this book is available from the British Library
Printed and bound in Great Britain.

who is SAS?

SAS is the world's largest privately held software company, providing organisations with the capability to derive intelligence from the wealth of data that is available to them. We provide the technology and know how to capitalise on your key investment.

SAS is used by more than 40,000 business, government and university sites, in 111 different countries and is the market leader for business intelligence. These organisations represent:

- ☐ 97 of the top 100 companies on the 2004 Fortune 500 List
- ☐ 96 of the top 100 companies on the 2003 Fortune Global 500 List
- ☐ 97 companies of the top 100 of the 2003 Forbes Super 100 List

what can we do for you?

Getting ahead of the competition and staying there is a constant challenge – strategy can be copied, technology can be replicated, and staff can be poached. However, your data is unique to your business and as such can be the source of on-going competitive differentiation, if used to its full potential.

The demand for new systems that support business with key information shows no signs of slowing – regulatory compliance, improving customer profitability, optimising operations, the list seems endless.

SAS can provide a business with a complete picture of its business performance and offer insight into future direction, utilising leading edge predictive technology. SAS software solutions integrate data from business applications and relevant 'external' data sources, providing an easy and rapid route to business intelligence that is often complex in nature. The result is complete intelligence about the performance of your business.

SAS solutions are integrated by design to meet specific business needs, mitigating risk and giving a valuable return on investment.

CONTENTS

With SAS, the leader in business intelligence software...

Make breakthrough decisions. And make an impact.

Go beyond business intelligence with SAS®, the one software that delivers accurate information to everyone. So you can drive profits, reduce costs, manage risk and transform the way you do business. Now that SAS®9 has arrived, you can take advantage of our proven predictive analytics through a single, scalable platform that spans the enterprise. And interact with SAS by choosing the custom-tailored interface that fits the way you work. See for yourself by taking the free interactive tour on our website or contact us at **info.uk@suk.sas.com**

www.sas.com/breakthrough

 SAS·9

The Power to Know.

rules are not enough

**George Cox, outgoing Director General
Institute of Directors**

Over the past few years, corporate governance has come under increasingly intense scrutiny. It is not difficult to see why. When America's seventh largest company in terms of capitalisation suddenly collapses, amid a fraud scandal involving one of the world's leading auditors, the whole system by which western business operates begins to feel unsafe.

When the debacle is followed by a spate of other incidents, public confidence arguably sinks to new lows. After Enron came more scandals in the US and the shattering collapse of Parmalat in Italy.

Even the UK, widely acknowledged as a leader in the governance field, has been in trouble: a series of high-profile companies has faced shareholder protests over apparently unjustifiable payouts to directors; a once highly respected oil company has had to admit that it misled the market over its reserves.

Corporate malpractice and wrong-doing are not 'victimless crimes'. When companies fail, employees lose their jobs, creditors lose their money, individuals lose their savings and people lose their pensions.

If you cannot trust a company to act in its shareholders' interests, and if you cannot trust its accounts, how can you expect people to invest in it?

Modern capitalism – the model to which virtually the whole world now aspires – is totally dependent on high standards of governance.

'Governance' means rigorous supervision of the management of a company; it means ensuring that business is done competently, with integrity and with due regard for the interests of all stakeholders.

Good governance is, therefore, a mixture of regulation, structure, best practice and board competency.

Much of the recent attention has focused on rules, codes of practice or regulation. In the UK, we have had our Higgs review (following in the wake of reports by Cadbury, Greenbury and Hampel); in the US, we have had the far more draconian Sarbanes-Oxley Act; and similar reviews are in progress in virtually every other advanced western democracy. They all play a part in carrying the state of the art a further step forward.

In countries where the framework for corporate governance is crude, rule books are a prerequisite for progress. It is a mistake, though, to think that they are all that is needed. Having a highway code does not, of itself, make people good drivers.

In countries with longer established governance systems, the issue is much more one of spreading best practice and raising the levels of board capability.

That's certainly true in the UK, where general standards of integrity are high (at variance perhaps with public perception) and the principle of 'comply or explain' (endorsed by the Higgs review) creates a sensible basis for board/shareholder discussion.

With the right structure for good corporate governance in place, the focus shifts to the professional development of directors and to board performance. The question becomes: how can we build a culture of continuous improvement?

The pressures on boardrooms can only increase. Governance is not a problem that will ever be 'solved': business will grow more complex; directors will come under more scrutiny; expectations will rise.

And, as any company chairman or chief executive will tell you, the relationship with institutional shareholders is, as yet, far from ideal.

The following pages cannot pretend to be the final word on governance. But they are a very good guide to the current state of the art and best practice.

Every director – or aspiring director – whether executive or non-executive, should find them of value.

governance for competitive gain

Alastair Sim, Director of Strategy and Marketing, SAS

In response to the recent increase in corporate scandals and the threat of terrorism worldwide, new compliance regulations demand higher standards of corporate governance and reporting.

Recent examples such as Enron and Worldcom, which suffered the fate of bankruptcy, illustrate how the lack of accuracy and speed can considerably increase risk. In many instances businesses are still disadvantaged by their manual approach to planning, budgeting and consolidation. They fail to see the opportunities that lie within the business because of a 'silo' infrastructure and lack of a joined-up information strategy. Furthermore, global complexity stretches the CFO office capabilities in statutory reporting and consolidation by complex matrix-driven organisational structures.

All these factors foster an organisation that is blind to its fate. However, authorities have started to take action on this situation and new international accounting standards (IAS) as well as defined rules on boards' capabilities and imposed penalties (Sarbanes-Oxley Act) have come into effect.

In some cases, regulation is forcing the board of directors to fully appreciate the business's financial situation. Board directors are now under extreme scrutiny from investors and shareholders, who want to ensure there is transparency in the organisation. Basel II and Sarbanes-Oxley are two such key regulatory issues facing businesses today, and the numbers are increasing as there is an attempt to close loop-holes and minimise bad business practices.

Compliance does impose significant costs on businesses, especially on public companies, and can put a dampener on economic activity and initiative. However, it can be an investment in both risk management and growth. Integrated business and technology systems offer an opportunity to turn corporate necessity into business benefit. The upfront expense and resource allocation to comprehensive aggregation, management and scrutiny of data – imposed on businesses by compliance requirements and more broadly by corporate governance policies – can be translated into future profits. Since so much of the data for compliance is customer related, a company can drill down into a repository or analyse a scenario for compliance purposes – but it can do so much more over time for customer intelligence, transaction patterns and market analyses. Business leaders have to refocus on accuracy, speed, global complexity and risk. They need new solutions for integrating data from business functions in a holistic way across the enterprise.

In summary, the benefits of adopting a positive approach to corporate governance are clear. Recent studies carried out among the international business community have shown that, on average, companies with recognised effective corporate governance commanded a significant share price premium.

With a global economy that is still recovering, businesses must meet the demand for increased access to information from shareholders, partners, customers, the government and even employees. Staying competitive means company directors must transform the way they conduct business if they are to avoid a sharp decline in investor confidence.

focus on the UK

Patricia Peter, head of corporate governance at the IoD, charts the progression of UK corporate governance reports and codes and advises what they mean for company directors

In the IoD's Standards for the Board, published in the UK in 2001, the key purpose of a company board is:

"to seek to ensure the company's prosperity by collectively directing the company's affairs, whilst meeting the appropriate interests of shareholders and relevant stakeholders."

The board and the individuals comprising it are at the heart of the company. They sit between those who provide the capital and to whom they are accountable, and those who carry out the policies and decisions they make and who are therefore accountable to them. Corporate governance exists to provide a framework within which these relationships can operate effectively and the board can fulfil its key purpose.

the legal framework

The starting point for tracing governance in the UK is the system of company law. This is a statute-based law, further developed by the courts through precedent. At its heart are the main statutory provisions:

☐ Companies Act 1985

☐ Companies Act 1989

☐ Company Directors Disqualification Act 1986

EXECUTIVE SUMMARY

☐ a formalised approach to governance started with the Cadbury Report

☐ UK reports and codes follow the 'comply or explain' approach

☐ discretion needs to be exercised in the adoption of specific governance principles

The legal framework continues to evolve. In an effort to encourage disclosure of information of 'material' interest to investors, the government is legislating for an Operating and Financial Review (OFR). The OFR will be a narrative report by quoted companies made annually to shareholders. It will set out the main trends and factors underlying the company's past performance and shaping its future development (see box on opposite page) Consultation on the OFR proposals closed on 6 August 2004. The forthcoming regulations are proposed to relate to accounting periods beginning on or after 1 January 2005. This means that, as things stand, the first OFRs will be published in 2006.

In the same time frame companies listed on regulated EU stock exchanges are having to get to grips with international accounting standards and to prepare their consolidated accounts on the basis of International Financial Reporting Standards (IFRS). There will be significant changes from UK GAAP, but eventually it is the aim that in accordance with the mission statement of the International Accounting Standards Board (IASB) there will be "a single set of high quality, understandable and enforceable global accounting standards that require transparent and comparable information in general purpose financial statements."

the self-regulatory framework

Much of governance goes beyond legislation. Company law deals at length with the individual responsibilities of directors, but hardly mentions the board in its collective capacity. This vital aspect has been developed instead by those with a company and investment background. Since the early 1990s it has moved ever higher up the agenda for both directors and investors.

The start of a formalised approach to the governance of UK companies was the report of the Committee on the Financial Aspects of Corporate Governance (the Cadbury Report) to which was attached a Code of Best Practice. This was further developed through a series of reworkings including those of the Greenbury Committee, which made recommendations on executive pay.

In 1995, it was decided that previous governance recommendations should be reviewed and that new issues should be addressed, and the two brought together in a single code. The work was carried out under the chairmanship of

THE OPERATING AND FINANCIAL REVIEW (OFR)

An Operating and Financial Review (OFR) is a narrative report that concentrates on future strategies and plans, risks and opportunities, qualitative and intangible assets and business relationships. It should not be formulaic, but should include all aspects that the directors consider necessary for understanding the business.

Many quoted companies already produce an OFR voluntarily. As the practice developed, the Accounting Standards Board (ASB) issued guidance in the form of a Statement in 1993, which was revised in 2003. The Company Law Review (CLR) had noted that "compliance with the ASB guidance is patchy," and recommended a mandatory OFR for companies "of significant economic size".

In 2002, the OFR was taken up in the DTI's White Paper Modernising Company Law, which proposed a test of 'materiality' for the inclusion of certain items. In December 2002, a working group was established to draw up broad principles and practical guidance on whether an item is 'material'.

In May 2004, the government stated that it intended to introduce a mandatory OFR by means of a secondary legislation for quoted companies only for years beginning 1 January 2005. In this instance 'quoted' refers to GB registered companies with a full London Stock Exchange listing, plus those officially listed in an EEA State or the New York Stock Exchange or Nasdaq. This was to tie in with the timetable for implementation of the EU Accounts Modernisation Directive on directors' reports. It issued a consultation that closed on 6 August 2004. At the same time, the working group's report The Operating and Financial Review – Practical Guidance for Directors was published. (The term 'material' was dropped from the draft regulations.)

The proposals have not been welcomed universally. At the time of writing, it is not certain to what extent the proposals are to be amended. The principle of the OFR has been largely accepted; it is the practicalities of its implementation that are giving rise to concerns. Among the main objections are:

- [ ] the standard of care involved requires an onerous and time-consuming verification process. Both companies and their auditors are alarmed at this prospect

- [ ] the OFR should be forward looking. Going against the recommendations of the CLR, the government proposes that there should be no safe harbour provision for forecasts honestly and reasonably made, but which are not fulfilled

- [ ] references to the intended audience for OFR are ambiguous

- [ ] the timetable is unrealistic.

Sir Ronald Hampel and culminated in a report in January 1998, entitled Final Report: Committee on Corporate Governance. This culminated in the Combined Code in June 1998.

In June 2002, Derek Higgs was asked by the DTI to look at the role and effectiveness of non-executive directors. He reported in January 2003, with suggested amendments to the Combined Code. In July 2003 the revised Combined Code was published, and took effect for reporting periods beginning on or after 1 November 2003. The Financial reporting Council (FRC) is now the guardian of the Combined Code, and intends to ensure that it maintains its relevance.

All the UK reports and codes have taken the 'comply or explain' approach – something that companies and directors guard jealously. It is apparent that much of the investment community also appreciates that it has the capacity to provide more dynamic and relevant governance than a rules-based approach. Although only quoted companies (those with a full London Stock Exchange listing) are obliged to report whether they comply with the Combined Code and, where they do not, explain their departures from its provisions, the Code has had a noticeable wider impact on governance. This is true not just of non-quoted companies, but also of organisations outside the commercial corporate sector where parallel codes of governance are emerging.

what should you be doing?

Whatever the type or size of the organisation, individual directors need to make sure that they're clear about the purpose of the board (as set out above), and their role in fulfilling it. Much has been written about board functions, but, in essence, most authorities agree that the board should:

☐ provide leadership in terms of the visions and values of the organisation

☐ determine strategies and structures for the organisation

☐ delegate to management

☐ exercise accountability to shareholders and be responsible to relevant stakeholders

The first principle of the Combined Code states that: "Every company should have an effective board". The board's effectiveness is widely regarded as a prerequisite for sustained corporate success. The quality and effectiveness of directors determines the quality and effectiveness of the board. Formal

MAIN PRINCIPLES OF THE COMBINED CODE

Section 1: companies

A   DIRECTORS

☐ A.1 the board
Every company should be headed by an effective board, which is collectively responsible for the success of the company

☐ A.2 chairman and chief executive
There should be a clear division of responsibilities at the head of the company between the running of the board and the executive responsibility for the running of the company's business. No one individual should have unfettered powers of decision

☐ A.3 board balance and independence
The board should include a balance of executive and non-executive directors (and, in particular, independent non-executive directors) such that no individual or small group of individuals can dominate the board's decision making

☐ A.4 appointments to the board
There should be a formal, rigorous and transparent procedure for the appointment of new directors to the board

☐ A.5 information and professional development
The board should be supplied in a timely manner with information in a form and of a quality appropriate to enable it to discharge its duties. All directors should receive an induction on joining the board and should regularly update and refresh their skills and knowledge

☐ A.6 performance evaluation
The board should undertake a formal and rigorous annual evaluation of its own performance and that of its committees and individual directors

☐ A.7 re-election
All directors should be submitted for re-election at regular intervals, subject to continued satisfactory performance. The board should ensure planned and progressive refreshing of the board

☐ a strengthened role for the audit committee in monitoring the integrity of the company's financial reporting, reinforcing the independence of the external auditor and reviewing the management of financial and other risks

B   REMUNERATION

☐ B.1 the level and make-up of remuneration
Levels of remuneration should be sufficient to attract, retain and motivate directors of the quality required to run the company successfully, but a company should avoid paying more than is necessary for this purpose. A significant proportion of directors' remuneration should be structured so as to link rewards to corporate and individual performance

THE COMBINED CODE

☐ B.2 procedure
There should be a formal and transparent procedure for developing policy on executive remuneration and for fixing the remuneration packages of individual directors. No directors should be involved in deciding his or her own remuneration

C ACCOUNTABILITY AND AUDIT

☐ C.1 financial reporting
The board should present a balanced and understandable assessment of the company's position and prospects

☐ C.2 internal control
The board should maintain a sound system of internal control to safeguard shareholders' investment and the company's assets

☐ C.3 audit committee and auditors
The board should establish formal and transparent arrangements for considering how they should apply the financial reporting and internal control principles and for maintaining an appropriate relationship with the company's auditors

D RELATIONS WITH SHAREHOLDERS

☐ D.1 dialogue with institutional shareholders
There should be a dialogue with shareholders based on the mutual understanding of objectives. The board as a whole has a responsibility for ensuring that a satisfactory dialogue with shareholders takes place

☐ D.2 constructive use of AGM
The board should use the AGM to communicate with investors and to encourage their participation

Section 2

E INSTITUTIONAL SHAREHOLDERS

☐ E.1 dialogue with companies
Institutional shareholders should enter into a dialogue with companies based on the mutual understanding of the objectives

☐ E.2 evaluation of governance disclosures
When evaluating a company's governance arrangements, particularly those relating to board structure and composition, institutional shareholders should give due weight to all relevant factors drawn to their attention

☐ E.3 shareholder voting
Institutional shareholders have a responsibility to make considered use of their votes

processes for appointment, induction and development should be adopted. Effectiveness of the board and its individual members has to be assessed. Increasingly, empirical measures for assessment are being adopted (see chapter 9).

balancing power

Since the board's roles are carried out by a group of individuals who together have collective responsibility, individual knowledge, experience and traits are vitally important. Much of the governance framework in the UK is devoted to ways in which those to whom the board is accountable can assess the suitability of the individuals for the role. The Combined Code states that no one individual should have unfettered powers of decision-making. It sets out how this can be avoided by splitting the roles of chairman and chief executive, and specifies what the role of the chairman should be.

The next task is to introduce safeguards against allowing an individual, or small group of individuals, to become dominant. Again, the Combined Code offers valuable guidance on the ratio of non-executive to executive directors and definitions of independence.

exercising discretion

Governance is about creating a framework to enable companies to create prosperity within margins that are recognised and understood by their share-holders. At the most basic level, it is about complying with structural requirements. Much of the Combined Code sets out structural norms that are underpinned by a business reason. It is the role of the board to assess the underlying business reasons and then determine whether it is in the best interests of its shareholders for that company at that time to adhere to the structural requirement in question. If it determines that it is not, it must be able to give a convincing explanation.

In the end, one has to come back to the purpose of the board: to provide the leadership to create prosperity. Leadership can only come about if the directors individually and collectively are of the appropriate calibre, with the necessary skills and experience to contribute effectively to the decision-making process.

global governance

Kerrie Waring, international professional development manager at the IoD, looks at key developments in corporate governance around the world

Over recent years, a series of high-profile companies have experienced spectacular collapses in their share prices and substantially eroded market and public confidence. Behind the Enron, Worldcom and Parmalat headlines has been the same basic story: bad governance.

EXECUTIVE SUMMARY

☐ global corporate governance initiatives are taking place

☐ legal and regulatory standards are increasing

☐ company performance and compliance is being measured

☐ board independence and effectiveness is in the spotlight

☐ shareholders are encouraged to become more engaged

Today, there are renewed calls for improved integrity and oversight of management, greater use of internal and external audit functions, higher levels of disclosure and transparency and greater engagement of institutional investors.

International bodies, governments, financial institutions, public and private sector organisations are encouraging corporate governance debate and spearheading initiatives on a national, regional and global scale. Better regulatory and non-regulatory corporate governance frameworks and enforcement mechanisms are being implemented through tougher company legislation and non-mandatory corporate governance codes.

encouraging dialogue and initiatives for reform

Multilateral organisations such as the World Bank and the Organisation for Economic Co-operation and Development (OECD) have been convening joint regional corporate governance roundtables over the past four years. During this time, around 25 meetings have been organised in almost 20 countries representing the five regions of Asia, Russia, Latin America, Eurasia and Southeast Europe. The meetings have raised the awareness of corporate governance and pushed the reform agenda forward, creating a framework for policy dialogue. They have also provided a forum for consultation with non-member OECD countries on the recently revised Principles of Corporate Governance (2004) that have been developed to assist governments in their efforts to evaluate and improve their frameworks of corporate governance.

In 2001, the World Bank and the OECD established the Global Corporate Governance Forum (GCGF) to meet the growing demand for governance reform worldwide. The GCGF has been identifying priorities for corporate governance reform, developing action plans, and leading initiatives in developing markets and emerging economies. One such initiative led by the Institute of Directors in the UK, involved the creation of a toolkit entitled 'Building Director Training Organisations' that aims to distil international experience on how to establish an organisation that can assist in the improved professionalism of directors.

underpinning the corporate governance framework

Most countries rely on a combination of legislative, regulatory and self-regulatory processes to underpin corporate governance practices. Company law provides the framework for corporate governance and is often reinforced for public companies listed on a stock exchange through listing rules. In addition national codes recommend voluntary best practice measures by which companies should abide.

Many countries have implemented appropriate legal and regulatory mechanisms to suit business, political and cultural norms but the level of enforcement of such mechanisms differs greatly. In many lesser-developed countries, lack of enforcement can be a major obstacle, with few legal actions pursued. With this in mind, the new OECD principles include a principle stating: "The corporate governance framework should promote transparent and efficient markets, be consistent with the rule of law and clearly articulate the division of responsibilities among different supervisory, regulatory and enforcement authorities."

regulation and codes of corporate governance

There is a growing proliferation of national codes, standards and guidelines. These are often based loosely on the OECD principles and are designed to promote the importance of properly functioning boards.

The OECD Principles of Corporate Governance are non-binding and have been deliberately designed to cover broad aspects of corporate governance, which can be adapted to the specific legal, economic and social circumstances of individual countries and regions.

The principles provide guidance for regulators, financial markets, corporations and other parties on:

☐   the basis for an effective corporate governance framework

☐   the rights of shareholders and key ownership functions

☐   the equitable treatment of shareholders

☐   the role of stakeholders in corporate governance

☐   disclosure and transparency

☐   the responsibilities of the board

In some cases, the development of a national code has followed a crisis in the corporate or banking sector. In others, there's been more general recognition of the need to assist legislative and regulatory authorities in their corporate governance reform efforts.

Often code development is initiated by government through a committee – as in the case of the UK's Combined Code of Corporate Governance. In other countries, it is entirely private-sector led, such as the 1992 and 2002 King reports, which outlined the standards for South Africa.

legislative reform

Legislation governing companies is generally enshrined in Company Law and statutory Acts. The US Sarbanes-Oxley Act 2002 (SOX), which extends to companies with a listing in the US, is having a dramatic effect after being drafted in response to the Enron and Worldcom scandals. It imposes criminal sanctions on chief executive officers and chief financial officers who knowingly sign off false financial statements. As a consequence, any company listed in the US is faced with increased administrative costs to comply with SOX.

There is a concern that this will deter some companies from listing – or encourage others to de-list. That said, SOX has encouraged a move to enhance transparency as a much needed response to corporate scandals for the benefit of companies and shareholders alike.

EU-level initiatives

In May 2003, the EU Commission issued a communication to the EU Council and the European Parliament entitled Modernising Company Law and Enhancing Corporate Governance in the European Union – A Plan to Move Forward (the Company Law Action Plan). It states that the EU "must define its own European corporate governance approach".

Although the report did not propose an EU-wide corporate governance code, it stated that "some specific rules and principles need to be agreed at EU level".

The EU Commission has divided the work into short, medium and long-term areas and proposes that the short-term objectives are achieved between 2003-2005. The following areas are suggested as targets for legislation:

- ☐ disclosure requirements
- ☐ exercise of voting rights
- ☐ cross-border voting
- ☐ enhanced disclosure by institutional investors
- ☐ enhancing responsibilities of board members

INTERNATIONAL ACCOUNTING STANDARDS

The International Accounting Standards Board (IASB) and its predecessors have been responsible over the last 30 years for the development of what were International Accounting Standards (IAS) and have now become International Financial Reporting Standards (IFRS).

These are soon to assume a new impact and importance. For accounting periods commencing on or after 1 January 2005, all companies listed on a regulated stock exchange in the EU (some 7,000 companies) will have to prepare their consolidated financial statements based on IFRS. Since this requirement extends to comparative figures, the changeover is already a reality.

Along with domestic standards of the 24 member states, UK GAAP will be consigned to history for these accounts. It is also looking likely that subsidiary and associated companies of listed companies will have to apply consolidated information based on IFRS, and other companies are permitted to do so.

In addition to the EU member states, there are some 70 other countries that will require or permit companies to adopt IFRS. The UK Accounting Standards Board (ASB) has stated that it will make a concerted effort to bring UK GAAP into line with IFRS, so that UK companies are not faced two sets of wholly different accounting standards. It has also pledged not to issue new standards that are more demanding or more restrictive than IFRS.

Companies will notice differences in the treatment of items in the following:

- [ ] deferred tax
- [ ] finance leasing
- [ ] financial instruments, especially derivatives and investments at fair values
- [ ] goodwill amortisation
- [ ] hedge accounting
- [ ] investment properties
- [ ] merger accounting
- [ ] pension costs for defined-benefit schemes
- [ ] preference shares and convertible bonds
- [ ] proposed dividends

Currently, the global reach of IFRS is in doubt, since the US is not among the 70 countries proposing to adopt it. However, there is a project afoot between the IASB and the Financial Accounting Standards Board (FASB) in the US to produce a standard that would have precisely the same wording in both Europe and the US. Until this happens, there will continue to be two main standards: IFRS and US GAAP. The SEC is in favour of convergence, and the IASB sees it as its top priority. In the meantime, it is anticipated that an exposure draft on business combinations will be published in early 2005.

duties and responsibilities of the board

Today, there is increased scrutiny on the role and effectiveness of board directors – both executive and non-executive. While global recommendations for an increased number of independent non-executive directors are widely accepted, there is also concern over the availability of individuals who fulfil new 'independence' criteria. On top of this, added time pressure and increased threats of litigation are deterring high quality candidates from taking board positions.

There is more emphasis on the need for continuous professional development of directors. This is increasing the role of national institutes of directors as training providers. Today, the IoD model is replicated in many countries to assist corporate governance reform. This proliferation has led the IoD to co-operate with other leading bodies to create a 'global director development circle' (GDDC). This aims to be the internationally recognised association for organisations aiming to meet the development needs of directors through research, education, dialogue and advocacy.

evaluation of performance and compliance

The FTSE Group, a UK company owned by the Financial Times and the London Stock Exchange, has recently announced that it is working with Institutional Shareholder Services (ISS), a US-based corporate governance services agency, to develop a new set of indices for investors. The FTSE/ISS corporate governance indices will provide a tool for global investors to identify companies' corporate governance performance. They will measure:

- ☐ the structure and independence of the board
- ☐ the independence and integrity of the audit process
- ☐ shareholder rights and protections
- ☐ remuneration systems for executive and non-executive directors
- ☐ executive and non-executive stock ownership

On a macro level, the World Bank and the International Monetary Fund are jointly preparing Reports of the Observance of Standards and Codes (ROSCs) and measuring how countries relate to the OECD's Principles of Corporate Governance. To date, around 20 countries have had assessments produced against a template including a capital market overview.

increased shareholder participation

It is not just the responsibilities and performance of directors that are under scrutiny. For many developed countries, ownership patterns have changed dramatically over the past decade with less individual share ownership, increased foreign investments and more collective institutional shareholding, such as those from pension funds and insurance companies. This is particularly so in the UK and the US where institutional investors are becoming increasingly active and are influencing board decisions in areas such as directors' remuneration, nomination and service contracts.

In the US, Michael Eisner, chief executive of Disney, was recently stripped of the company chairmanship after shareholder pressure. And it was UK shareholders who, in 2003, threw out the remuneration report in respect of Jean Pierre Garnier's pay at GlaxoSmithKline. There have also been high profile resignations through shareholder pressure. They include the infamous departure from the New York Stock Exchange of Dick Grasso of the New York Stock Exchange who bowed to pressure predominantly from Calpers, a Californian State Employees Pension Fund with over $170bn worth of assets.

There is far less shareholder influence in companies based in developing countries. In many situations, majority shareholders with a high degree of control through family holdings, have a significant effect on minority shareholder rights. Often controlling shareholders can extract private benefits from a company at the expense of other shareholders who can do little to stop frequent abuse.

The level of government control within the corporate sector in emerging markets is also a significant factor. The private sector is often very small and the most significant industries are state owned. In South Africa, for example, the state controls around a quarter of the country's capital stock. Heavy state influence raises questions about the independence of directors as many are often political appointments. Many countries are now using the OECD Principles of

Corporate Governance as a guide for improving the rights and equitable treatment of minority shareholders.

ongoing improvement

Some of the key issues surrounding corporate governance in developing markets have been succinctly described in a series of OECD White Papers on Corporate Governance published for Russia, Asia, Southeast Europe and Latin America. They have been developed to identify common policy objectives and key areas for reform.

A well-functioning board is key to the performance of companies and their capacity to attract capital. A well-established corporate governance framework should ensure that boards monitor managerial performance effectively to achieve an equitable return for shareholders and uphold the values of fairness, transparency, accountability and responsibility.

SAS, the leader in business intelligence software, challenges…

Regulatory compliance. Shareholder value.
Are you delivering both?

OPERATIONAL RISK

CREDIT RISK

COMPLIANCE

MARKET RISK

Basel II. Sarbanes-Oxley. Regulatory requirements keep growing. So do stakeholder expectations. And both are forcing you to gain a new understanding of every part of your business. SAS software delivers that enterprise view, combining nearly three decades of analytic accuracy and market leadership in one incomparable risk management suite. So you can adapt quickly to regulatory and stakeholder demands. To learn more about SAS, and our real-world successes, visit our Web site or contact us at info.uk@suk.sas.com

www.sas.com/risk

With SAS you can aggregate data in any volume from across your enterprise. Model and predict likelihood and impact. And approach credit, operational and market risk with consistency and proven reliability.

 SAS 9

The Power to Know. |  §sas.

governance as strategy

European companies have generally been far too passive about governance. Business ethics lecturer and author Alan Malachowski shows how they can put this right by seizing the strategic initiative

It will probably take many more years to figure out the significance of the recent corporate scandals. But, post-Enron and co., one thing is becoming very clear already: too many companies have been too slow in recognising the strategic importance of good governance.

KPMG has recently carried out international research among chief financial officers and financial directors which shows that many companies are actively supporting the current widespread initiatives to improve governance. However, while 44 per cent of respondents claimed 'achieving genuine improvements' was the key driving factor in their organisation's approach to governance, very few made any definite connections with their strategic aims. Only six per cent, for example, revealed that their main goal was 'maximising share price'.

Fortunately, further empirical research is starting to confirm what ought to be a matter of plain common sense: the practices and processes of governance make good business sense and can be value-enhancing in themselves. In other words, companies that have the foundations of proper governance

EXECUTIVE SUMMARY

- [ ] current research on attitudes to governance shows lack of focus on its strategic potential

- [ ] governance requirements should be assessed for the possibility of strategic fit

- [ ] the board needs to aim for a level of governance that pre-empts the need for external interference

- [ ] recent strategic developments in corporate philanthropy provide a model for changing perspective on governance

in place are usually a much better bet for investors than those that ignore this fundamental requirement (see chapter 3). Nevertheless, the 'strategic premium' that effective governance can yield is always likely to outstrip the benefits currently envisaged by such research.

outside the box

Good governance involves much more than the box ticking exercises that many directors regard as an intrusive prelude to their real work in any case. Since the Cadbury report, three areas of corporate governance have been emphasised in regulatory and media forums:

- ☐ board structure
- ☐ board activities
- ☐ compliance with prevailing codes

Of these, by first has received by far the most attention, especially after Higgs when inflammatory issues concerning the number and quality of non-executives caught the eye of the media. This has led to a corresponding neglect of the board's activities, and a consequent failure to grasp the importance of 'active governance'.

pro-active boards

The main activities of the board that involve issues of governance are:

- ☐ risk management
- ☐ assurance control
- ☐ supply and flow of information

In each of these cases, there is plenty of scope for directors to take initiatives that go beyond habitual 'compliance for compliance's sake' and thereby generate strategic pay-offs.

The secret of strategic success is to be both pro-active and innovative. Take, for example, the third category of board activities: supply and flow of information.

The primary informational task of the board is two-fold:

- [ ] to ensure that the directors' deliberations are based on timely, high quality information

- [ ] to facilitate the external flow of accurate information so that investors, analysts and the quality business media are suitably well-informed about the company's actual performance and its future prospects

A pro-active board will carefully examine all those formal governance requirements that concern information to determine whether these requirements can be turned to the company's competitive advantage. Mere compliance is too passive.

An international study by investor relations consulting firm Blunn and Company shows that most public companies still fail to provide even the most basic governance information on their corporate web sites. "It is clear from the survey that companies need to do more to communicate the corporate governance and internal control changes they have been making in the wake of corporate scandals and new regulations. They may be making important improvements, but they are largely doing so behind closed doors without keeping the investment public informed," says Dominic Jones, the report's author.

Given this depressing news, it is fitting that, as part of its action plan Modernising Company Law and Enhancing Corporate Governance (see chapter 1, part two), the EU will require an 'annual corporate governance statement' in which companies have to outline the key components of their governance structures and practices. If the requirement comes into effect, a pro-active board will need to investigate whether their governance statement can be customised to demonstrate the company's business effectiveness to investors. Ideally, such a board would have already anticipated the demand for this kind of gesture and would be using it, innovatively, to its strategic advantage.

philanthropy: a comparison

The shift towards a proper strategic appreciation of governance practices could usefully mirror the swift awakening from strategic inertness that has occurred in the sphere of corporate philanthropy in the United States.

In the past, corporate charitable expenditure tended to be arbitrary. Money was invariably spent on piecemeal projects that CEOs and their PR people hoped would create good publicity for the organisation. Funds were not strategically targeted, and benefits were not meaningfully monitored. In short, good intentions outweighed good business sense.

Increasingly, however, US companies are now treating charitable expenditure like any other business investment. Following the recommendations of influential academic theorists such as Porter and Kramer (Harvard Business Review, 2002), they are using it to "improve their competitive context – the quality of the business environment in the location where they operate". In doing so, companies are starting to creatively synchronise economic and social goals in ways that improve their longer-term business prospects. This has the added bonus of enabling businesses to channel their unique commercial skills into their charitable deeds. They need no longer be left shooting from the hip in the philanthropic dark.

The Cisco Networking Academy, the brainchild of Cisco Systems, is a striking example of this new approach to charitable expenditure. It involves large-scale investment in an ambitious educational programme to train computer network administrators. This programme has the strategic benefit of forestalling a potentially damaging constraint on Cisco's future growth while, at the same time, providing attractive job opportunities to high school graduates and also improving community relations.

Pro-active and innovative boards both here in the UK and in Europe need to take a similar strategic leap with regard to methods of governance. Individual directors, and especially the chair person, should champion a level of governance practice that is designed to pre-empt codes, legislation and governmental interference in general. At a minimum, all mandatory, and probably most recommended, governance requirements should be studied in detail by the board, or one of its committees, to find out whether they exhibit any signs of 'strategic fit' (imagine what could have happened if accountancy firms had carried out this kind of exercise on 'assurance' requirements well before the scandals that rocked their industry). From then on, the focus for action is obvious.

If certain governance requirements turn out to have strategic merit (obviously not all will), then they should form the active core of the company's governance policy.

BEYOND RULES

In February 2004, Governance Metrics International, the renowned corporate governance research and ratings agency, awarded its highest overall rating of 10 to Pfizer for the third consecutive time. This assessment graphically confirmed the company's long-term commitment to the highest possible standards of corporate governance.

Pfizer has consistently taken a proactive approach to governance and thereby pre-empted the shock effects of regulatory interference. Long before Sarbanes Oxley and the New York Stock Exchange issued the rules and regulations that raised the bar in the sphere of governance, Pfizer had already been following the vast majority of the recommended guidelines for practice.

It had, for instance, always disclosed its processes of nominating directors and communicating with shareholders. Furthermore, its corporate governance principles and all three charters for the audit, compensation and corporate governance committees had been included in its proxy for many years. Pfizer's corporate governance web site introduced 'model' levels of transparency and accountability long before the current disclosure demands were put in place.

More recently, the company demonstrated how it anticipates changes in the formal environment of governance by implementing a two-day electronic filing of SEC Form 4s (officer and director purchase and sales of company stock) a year before the SEC made this a mandatory requirement.

Pfizer is also a good example of a company that is strategic in selecting governance policies that suit its particular commercial requirements. Thus it continues to resist the clarion call for a complete separation of the roles of Chairman and CEO. Pfizer defends its stance by appealing to its special need to navigate through a variety of special interests including those of 'shareholders, colleagues, and communities'. The company argues forcefully that such 'navigation' is best carried out by someone who is able to combine the roles of chairman and CEO. At the same time, Pfizer is pragmatic, admitting that its current stance is provisional, and that future circumstances may dictate a different outlook.

SAS, the leader in business intelligence software, demands...

The truth, the whole truth, and nothing but the truth

ENTERPRISE INTELLIGENCE

SUPPLIER INTELLIGENCE

ORGANISATIONAL INTELLIGENCE

CUSTOMER INTELLIGENCE

INTELLIGENCE PLATFORM

When different business functions deliver different versions of the truth, it's difficult to consolidate multiple reports into one reliable view. That makes it hard to focus on, or even identify, the critical metrics that provide transparency to ensure your business success. With the SAS Intelligence Platform, we're delivering the technology that will support a holistic view of performance management. We're also tailoring that view to your industry, building the major indicators that will impact your business into our intelligence solutions. What else would you expect from the world's leader in performance management software. To learn more about SAS visit our Web site or contact us on info.uk@suk.sas.com

www.sas.com/align

The Power to Know® |

the bottom line

Deutsche Bank recently carried out in-depth research into the impact of governance on financial performance. Gavin Grant, one of the analysts involved, explains the findings

Companies that are committed to the principles of good corporate governance offer the best opportunities for investors. Corporate governance should be a critical factor in investment decisions. Market valuations should reflect standards of governance systems and procedures.

These statements are not based on suppositions or wild hypotheses. The correlation between good governance and good business can be empirically proven. Deutsche Bank has analysed companies in the FTSE 350 index and back-tested its analysis over the past three years. It has found a clear link between standards of corporate governance and share-price performance, equity risk (ie. share-price volatility) and profitability measures (ie. return on equity, return on assets and EBITDA margin – the extent to which operating expenses use up revenue). Companies with the highest quality of governance structure and behaviour have outperformed those with the lowest.

governance criteria

When analysing companies, governance factors can be divided into four main groups.

board independence

We examine the board's ability to act independently from management in the best interests of all shareholders. We look at the structure of the board, its compositions and at its overall capabilities.

EXECUTIVE SUMMARY

- ☐ the link between good governance and business success is irrefutable
- ☐ companies with weak governance systems are significant investment risks
- ☐ many FTSE 350 companies are failing to adapt to new governance standards
- ☐ governance should be a key factor in analysts' recommendations

shareholder treatment

We address questions related to the treatment of minority shareholders. We also consider issues such as the company's capital structure and its impact on shareholder rights.

information disclosure

We look at the quality, extent and timeliness of information provided to analysts and investors. We also deal with the structure of company information (accounting standards and auditing relations) and internal verification mechanisms.

corporate compensation

We address both independent director and executive compensation, inquiring into the setting, monitoring and measurement of compensation. We look at the level of base salary and the various layers of bonuses and performance-related compensations and at the setting and disclosure of chief executive performance targets.

data points

Investors who have ploughed their way through annual reports, Stock Exchange filings and listing prospectuses, will know that there is no shortage of non-financial company information. From the hundreds of possible choices, we collect the 50 pieces of governance data that we believe are most relevant to institutional shareholders. Our information sources are: Pensions and Investments Research Consultants (PIRC), Bloomberg, Factset, the companies themselves and our own analysts.

scoring methodology

We divide the corporate governance 'facts' about a company into those of primary, secondary and tertiary importance to investors. A fourth category covers useful points of information. Primary, secondary and tertiary issues receive weighted scores.

Examples of the 'assessment hierarchy' include:

- [ ] primary issues: the independence of the chairman and of members of the remuneration, audit and nomination committees; equal voting rights for each ordinary share; directors' statement of compliance with the Combined Code

- [ ] secondary issues: contracts for directors that do not exceed one year; a requirement for directors to build up equity stakes

- [ ] tertiary issues: disclosure of maximum potential awards; right of the audit committee to engage outside advisers

- [ ] information issues: chief executive's share option gains; political contributions

controls on the research

Understanding that corporate governance structures and behaviour are by no means the only factors determining profitability, we analyse the relationship between governance and profitability at sector level.

We find that even when sector-specific issues are taken into account, the impact of corporate governance on profitability is clear.

results

The charts on pages 34 and 35 show some of our key, general findings. They might be summarised or supplemented by the following statements.

- [ ] investments in companies with the highest quality of governance structures and behaviour significantly outperform those with the lowest

- [ ] companies with the top 20 per cent of governance scores are more profitable than those within the bottom 20 per cent. While the bottom 20 per cent had an average return on equity (ROE) of 1.5 per cent in 2002, the top 20 per cent had an average ROE of 15.9 per cent the same year

- [ ] the higher the corporate governance score, the lower the equity-price volatility.

FTSE 350 EX-INVESTMENT TRUSTS

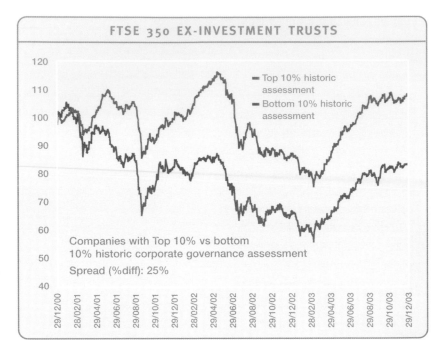

Companies with Top 10% vs bottom
10% historic corporate governance assessment

Spread (%diff): 25%

CORPORATE GOVERNANCE AND RETURN ON EQUITY

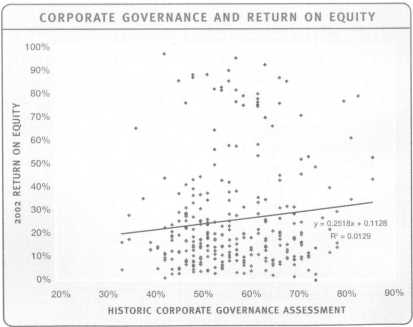

$y = 0.2518x + 0.1128$
$R^2 = 0.0129$

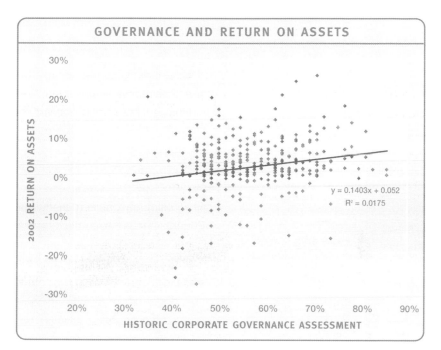

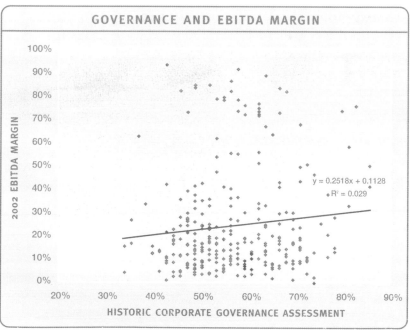

Source: Bloomberg, Deutsche Bank Securities Inc estimates and company information

the bigger picture

These facts and figures, however, do not tell the whole story. The analysis finds that standards of governance within the FTSE 350 vary from the near perfect to the far from perfect. Corporate governance assessments range from a high of 83 per cent to a low of 33 per cent. Additionally, we have identified a marked difference in the resolve of companies to adapt to new standards of best practice. The conclusion has to be that a worrying proportion of British companies are putting their futures – and that of their stakeholders – at risk.

The sectoral analyses reveal that some stocks are priced too high or too low when corporate governance factors are taken into account. Consider, for example, the assessments of the high-street jewellers Signet Group and the luxury-brand retailer Burberry Group. Signet shows similar profitability measures to Burberry while enjoying much better governance standards. In other words, it offers similar levels of profitability for a lower risk. Despite this, Signet trades at a discount to the sector average, Burberry at a premium. But Signet and Burberry are not alone. Several of the companies in the study may be termed valuation 'outliers'.

where next?

Deutsche Bank's hope is that its research will help shareholders not only to make more accurate assessments of investment risk but also to play an even more active role in corporate governance. With the right tools to measure governance standards, they will be able to anticipate governance risk – rather than merely react to it.

We also hope that the findings will lead to fairer market valuations, forcing corrections to 'false' discounts and premiums.

The message to investors is clear: corporate governance should be a key factor in your decision-making; assess your portfolios for corporate governance risk. The corollary is that companies must make concerted and consistent efforts to follow corporate governance best practice. If they don't, they could find themselves starved of capital.

CHAPTER 5

the price of failure

Carol Kennedy, management author, looks at the damage defective governance systems have done to once respected British companies

"You can be sure of Shell." The famous pre-war slogan has come back to haunt the dual boardrooms of Royal Dutch/Shell, where trust among investors and market analysts has evaporated as fast as the inflated oil reserves in the company's accounts.

In just a few months in 2004, one of the world's most admired companies became one of the most pilloried. Shell was perceived as guilty of three of the biggest sins in corporate governance: senior board incompetence, disastrous internal and external communications and 'reward for failure'. Even after the group's autocratic chairman, Sir Philip Watts, was forced to resign, the company still appeared willing to pay him five times his contractual entitlement.

As revelations seeped out week after week, including evidence that the Dutch supervisory board chairman knew of an 'imminent problem' with the reserves two months before disclosure (the UK chairman Lord Oxburgh denied prior knowledge), reform was being urged by some of Shell's biggest institutional investors, including the powerful California state pension fund (Calpers).

Shareholders wanted greater transparency and commitment to overhaul a Byzantine governance structure that included a two-tier Dutch board, a single-tier British board

EXECUTIVE SUMMARY

- [ ] it takes decades to build a good reputation but only months to lose it
- [ ] good governance anticipates problems and preserves public trust
- [ ] non-executives are increasingly held accountable for company failures
- [ ] investors will continue to exert pressure for reform

(each subject to different laws) and an executive committee of managing directors, two Dutch and one British.

One disillusioned investor said in the run-up to the group's stormy AGM in June: "We have got the impression that they want to get away with as little [in the way of transparency] as they can. It is a question of trust and the fact that trust has broken down."

when trust takes a beating

Shell is only one of several iconic companies where trust and reputation have been taking a beating because of things that could have been avoided or countered by good governance. Marks and Spencer, like Shell once famed for integrity and competence in its management culture, emerges as having been dysfunctional for years, questions over its board competence going back to the messy succession to Sir Richard Greenbury in 1999. Earlier in the 1990s, Shell seems to have destroyed its old proven matrix of management skills in a misguided attempt to make its culture more devolved and entrepreneurial.

When the M&S board finally appointed a respected top retailer, Stuart Rose, as chief executive, only to be caught up in an unwelcome bid from BHS chairman Philip Green, the story took a turn worthy of pulp fiction. There were reports of spying into Rose's mobile phone records, of Green and Rose being embroiled in a furious pavement row and, to top it all, a full-blown investigation by the Financial Services Authority (FSA) into allegations of insider share dealing by Rose.

Although the FSA swiftly cleared the new chief executive, the cumulative effect did not help to restore confidence in the one-time king of the high street after years of uncertain direction. "There has been reputational damage," says David McWilliam, senior consultant to the IoD on governance best practice. "The whole M&S story has been a corporate governance disaster."

Sainsbury is another fallen icon whose market decline since the invincible Lord (John) Sainsbury stepped down in 1992 has recently been compounded by disasters that anyone wise in corporate governance could have seen coming. The rushed appointment of Sir Ian Prosser to succeed chairman Sir Peter Davis, humiliatingly forced into reverse by shareholder objections; the subsequent sacking of Davis and yet another unseemly tussle over a golden payoff — all these have drawn scathing criticism, particularly of the Sainsbury non-executives. Only Lord Levene, who apparently took the lead in confronting Davis, came out with any credit. "This was clearly a dysfunctional board," said one institutional investor, speaking of the nomination and remuneration committees. "The non-executives didn't seem involved."

'the author of its own misfortunes'

Worst of all, in its destruction of countless pension incomes, was the misgovernance of Equitable Life, which blew a £4.4bn hole in the mutual's accounts, caused by years of excess payouts to earlier policy holders. A report by the Scottish judge Lord Penrose excoriated the society's management for being "the author of its own misfortunes". It personally criticised Roy Ranson, chief executive from 1991 to 1997, for being "autocratic", "manipulative", "obstructive" and "frequently aggressive in his dealings with regulators".

Penrose said the board had failed to scrutinise with sufficient robustness the practices that had led to Equitable's near-collapse, but he reserved particular condemnation for the non-executives, whom he accused of being "incompetent" and without enough knowledge of life-company accounts to challenge Ranson effectively. In future, Penrose recommended, non-executives of life companies should take direct personal responsibility for actuarial decisions.

Fifteen Equitable Life directors face trial in 2005 for their alleged role in helping to bring the 241-year-old insurance society to the brink of insolvency. Nine former non-executives, including former Millennium Dome chief executive Jennie Page and Peter Sedgwick, former chairman of fund managers Schroders, had appealed in vain for the case to be dismissed, arguing that the allegations were seriously flawed. The same trial is expected to encompass a multi-billion-pound lawsuit by Equitable itself against its former auditors, Ernst and Young.

The Equitable case is likely to have far-reaching implications for governance, including Penrose's recommendation that non-executives accept actuarial responsibility. The nine non-executives who sought to have the case against them dismissed said failure was a blow to hopes of encouraging a wider range of non-executives into British boardrooms. Tighter liability over financial reporting, already signalled in the US by the Sarbanes-Oxley legislation and spreading into the European Union, might have a similar deterrent effect.

public opinion matters

A key lesson from these dented corporate reputations is that companies can no longer afford to take a dismissive view of shareholder – and indeed public – opinion, or to appear arrogant in dealing with the world outside their boardrooms. The issue of excessive pay packages is causing shareholder revolts – most spectacularly at pharmaceutical group GSK in 2003, where investors defied the board in voting down a £22m severance package for CEO Jean-Pierre Garnier.

Jarvis, the contractor that once dominated railway maintenance, lost business following the Potters Bar rail crash and has recently seen its share price in freefall. Some think its misfortunes might have been tempered had its board behaved differently after the disaster. "They came across as very defensive and unsympathetic to the bereaved families," says McWilliam. "It did them a lot of damage."

"There has been widespread change in the way investors regard large companies, and far greater publicity is now given to this kind of issue," McWilliam adds. "Companies need to think much more about what reactions are going to be from shareholders and other stakeholders, and not assume that decisions will be accepted just because they are honest, which most companies are, and full of highly intelligent people. These were all avoidable mistakes."

image issues for bigger companies

Professor Bernard Taylor of Henley Management College, which runs courses for plc board members, says investors are moving much more towards active "engagement" with the companies in which they place their money.

"At the moment, people do not trust big companies, and companies have to take this very seriously," says Taylor.

Pollsters including MORI have consistently shown that 70-80 per cent of the population believe leaders of big companies are not to be trusted. There is a perception that they are primarily interested in lining their own pockets rather than, for example, honouring obligations to pensioners.

In the UK, says Taylor, "there is quite a significant move towards more independent boards, tougher regulations, more shareholder power, an angry press." Despite this, he does not detect a 'general surge' towards director training in better governance.

"On the whole, people in large companies are not aware how much their customers are alienated from them," he says.

So what will force the necessary change? Taylor comes back to the issue of shareholder 'engagement'. "Companies act not because of codes or personal reputation," he argues, "they act only when a threat comes from investors."

managing risk
part one: developing a strategy

> Risk management is synonymous with corporate governance. Peyman Mestchian, director, risk management practice, SAS UK, looks at how to do it properly

The Stock Exchange's Combined Code on Corporate Governance places much emphasis on the need to manage risk. Principle C.2 states that "The board should maintain a sound system of internal control to safeguard shareholders' investment and the company's assets"; a 13-page annexe, added to the Code after the publication of the Turnbull report in 1999, offers guidance on how this principle might be applied.

Risk management, though, is far more than a regulatory requirement. Beneath the rubric lies a stark reality: without the ability to control and manage risks effectively no company, whether public or private, will be in business for long.

EXECUTIVE SUMMARY

- [ ] the sensible company takes risks – but not gambles
- [ ] risk identification processes must be comprehensive
- [ ] each member of the organisation must be empowered to treat risk
- [ ] companies need robust systems for collecting risk-related data

what is good risk management?

Put very simply, effective risk management is about taking risks responsibly.

It is usually seen as consisting of three inter-related disciplines:

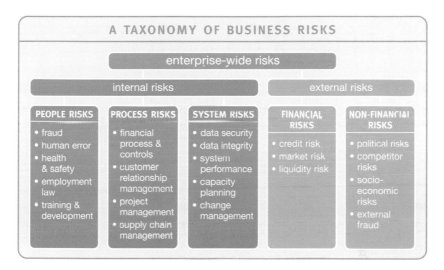

A TAXONOMY OF BUSINESS RISKS

enterprise-wide risks

internal risks			external risks	
PEOPLE RISKS	**PROCESS RISKS**	**SYSTEM RISKS**	**FINANCIAL RISKS**	**NON-FINANCIAL RISKS**
• fraud • human error • health & safety • employment law • training & development	• financial process & controls • customer relationship management • project management • supply chain management	• data security • data integrity • system performance • capacity planning • change management	• credit risk • market risk • liquidity risk	• political risks • competitor risks • socio-economic risks • external fraud

☐ risk identification

☐ risk assessment/analysis

☐ risk mitigation

The sensible company acknowledges that risks are a fact of entrepreneurial life. But it does not take risks unknowingly. It thinks about all the things that could go wrong with a project or activity and looks at the probability of each happening. It calculates the likely impact of each risk on the organisation. It then develops strategies to cope and contingency plans, 'prioritising' its efforts in favour of those events that are likely to cause most damage, or lead to the greatest losses.

The process is complex. To be worthwhile, it must be comprehensive, focusing not just on narrow financial risks but also those, to quote from the Turnbull Guidance, "related to market, credit, liquidity, technological, legal, health, safety and environmental, reputation and business probity issues".

organisational risk management

At a more detailed level, risk management is about the effective use of resources through improved process efficiency, the establishment of a sound system of internal controls, the sharing of knowledge and good practice, and the leveraging

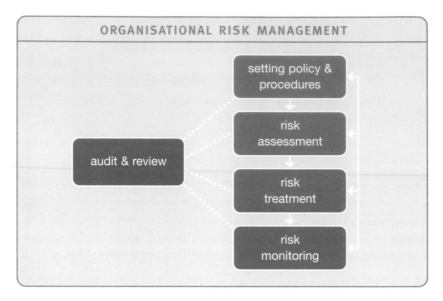

of technology to collect and analyse internal and external data.

It is also about supervision and review. Risk management systems should change as the company changes: controls can become redundant or anachronistic; business change is likely to bring new operational and 'process' risks.

risks and rewards

At the heart of good risk management activity is the 'risk-reward balance'. A company must weigh the potential risks associated with a decision against the potential rewards. This will mean recognising that, in some circumstances, doing nothing, taking no risks, might be an expensive mistake.

As Sir Nigel Turnbull said in a briefing at the IoD shortly after publishing his guidelines on internal control: "While the automatic reaction of many people to the word 'risk' is the need to reduce it, a more important risk for many businesses is the failure to respond, for example, by allowing a new product to be produced late or by failing to widen the customer base or prepare for e-commerce".

Most strategic decisions will be 'speculative risks', taken in the reasonable expectation of business benefits or reward.

managing 'pure risks'

'Pure risks' such as fire, theft, vandalism and accidental damage can be insured against. It is important, though, that the insurance policy does not become a risk-management substitute. Staff need to be educated in the importance of health and safety issues and security issues, and encouraged to take care of business-critical equipment. Insurance claims are undesirable – a business risk in themselves.

what is poor risk management?

Poor management of risk can have a negative impact on the achievement of business objectives and, ultimately, shareholder value. This can materialise in a number of ways:

- ☐ direct losses: project failures, litigation costs, irrecoverable asset or fund transfer, unexpected staff costs, regulatory penalties, physical damage and theft, interruptions in the supply chain, breaks in business continuity

- ☐ indirect losses: brand-value erosion or reputational damage, loss of market share, loss of key staff, loss of key customers, increased insurance costs

- ☐ opportunity costs: lost opportunities to enter new markets or develop new products, to leverage the latest technologies, to gain a competitive edge

practical challenges

Organisations are faced with many practical challenges on the way to developing effective organisational systems and functions for risk management.

One of them is data collection. Current and historic financial data, qualitative assessments by management, key risk indicators derived from internal operation and performance systems, information on high-impact, low-probability events – all these and more are needed for the effective management of risk.

Companies must have robust internal reporting procedures as well as the IT to support them.

A COMPANY PERSPECTIVE

Trying to fulfil sector-specific regulations within the wider context of corporate governance can be tough, says Bill Tonks, divisional director (risk management), Nationwide building society

Broadly speaking, the regulatory regime for retail finance services is operated by the Financial Services Authority. It seeks to deliver levels of business conduct and financial integrity that, so far as is reasonable and practicable in a free economy, protects the interests of consumers, and ensures that markets and the wider financial infrastructure are orderly, competitive and free from financial crime.

The institutional structures driving financial services are relatively mature and well defined. Firms know, more or less, where regulation will come from and expect a reasonable level of consistency in its formulation and application.

By contrast, corporate governance is still evolving, with input from a number of sources. As a result, aligning organisations' responses to the imperatives of corporate governance and regulation can be difficult as the different dynamics that drive the two regimes make themselves felt.

Another potential area of tension in financial services is the relation between the collective responsibility inherent in many areas of corporate governance – which requires committee structures to discharge it – and the individual management accountability now explicit in the FSA's regulatory system. Under each regime, who is responsible for what is clear. However, when structures and accountability systems developed for one regime are viewed from the point of view of the other, this clarity can break down.

There are also practical consequences to be dealt with. In pursuit of good governance, most organisations split day-to-day responsibilities in such a way that the pulling together of compliance regimes is not always easy. Even tackling simple matters such as the length and complexity of 'board days' and the running of secretariat functions begin to eat up significant chunks of executive time.

There is a danger that the load of compliance, and its disjunctive nature, will make line management feel hounded and begin to cause incoherence in the control and risk management structure of organisations. Even 'good governance' models may begin to break down as the rational distribution of functions and workloads is found to be inconsistent with some requirements.

There is always the danger that prescriptive regimes promote form over function, and thus they should be avoided. As Sir Howard Davis observed, when both chairman and chief executive of the FSA, it is character in boards, not structure, that delivers effective governance and appropriate and effective compliance.

risk-management solutions

The importance and complexity of risk management has spawned a multi-million pound 'service' industry. Everyone from audit and consulting firms and insurance firms to software companies wants to help companies get it right, and a proliferation of tools and techniques is now on the market.

what should you look for in a supplier?

Credible consultants and 'specialists' will probably acknowledge four key principles of risk management. It:

- ☐ is a process
- ☐ belongs to everyone in the firm
- ☐ requires qualitative and quantitative data
- ☐ needs sponsorship from the top

Do not believe anyone who gives the impression that risk management can be 'bought in' or overlaid on existing processes. As the Turnbull Guidance says, it must "be embedded in the operations of the company and form part of its culture".

One of the best organisational risk-management solutions, then, is employee communication and employee education. Each individual within the organisation must be empowered to identify, assess and treat the risks within their sphere of control.

part two: adding value

Dr Neville Bain, chairman of the audit committee at Scottish & Newcastle PLC, discusses how the audit committee can ensure that good governance adds value to the business

Following the proliferation of reports and codes there is a danger that governance is beginning to be regarded as too prescriptive and, in many cases, destroying shareholder value. The unsurprising consequence of this is that boards are becoming pre-disposed to 'ticking boxes' and 'doing the right thing', rather than focusing on ensuring that good governance adds value. The focus of this chapter is therefore about adding value rather than specific legal obligations.

EXECUTIVE SUMMARY

- ☐ good governance is about more than ticking boxes or doing the right thing
- ☐ the scope and objectives of the audit committee need to be seen as integral to the overall aims of the board
- ☐ the chairman must secure a good relationship with the directors and key executives of the business
- ☐ it is the job of the audit committee to ensure that external auditors fulfil the needs of the business

audit and risk

Many organisations have broadened the title of the audit committee to 'audit and risk', reflecting the wider role and importance of risk assessment and control as a fundamental foundation.

Risk assessment and control process need not only to be embedded in the organisation but also to be subject to regular review by the executive board. Evaluation is best achieved in interactive workshops, preferably with an outside facilitator. The results are then refined and reported to the board and regularly reviewed. Those organisations using the 'balanced scorecard' reporting will have the high level risks included in this.

AUDIT COMMITTEE: COMPOSITION AND ROLE

Following the major corporate failures in the US in 2002, Sir Robert Smith, chairman of the Weir Group, was asked to chair an independent group to clarify the role and responsibilities of audit committees and to develop the existing Combined Code guidance.

The key points reflected in the revised Combined Code, published on 24 July 2003, were:

composition

The board should:

☐ establish an audit committee of at least three members, all independent non-executive directors

☐ satisfy itself that at least one member has significant, recent and relevant financial experience

☐ provide suitable training to committee members on an ongoing and timely basis

role

The role of the committee is:

☐ to monitor the integrity of the financial statements of the company, reviewing significant financial reporting judgements

☐ to review the company's internal financial control system and risk management systems, unless the latter is expressly addressed by a separate risk committee or the board

☐ to monitor and review the effectiveness of the company's internal audit function

☐ to make recommendations to the board in relation to the external auditor's appointment; in the event of the board rejecting the recommendation, the committee and the board should explain their respective positions in the annual report

☐ to monitor and review the external auditor's independence, objectivity and effectiveness, while taking into consideration relevant UK professional and regulatory requirements

☐ to develop and implement policy on the engagement of the external auditor to supply non-audit services, taking into account relevant ethical guidance regarding the provision of non-audit services by the external audit firm

Smith report

The Smith Report was sensible and codified best practice. However, it is a template, which should be tested against the particular needs of a particular organisation, rather than slavishly followed in the name of compliance.

A few of Smith's recommendations are worth commenting on. In particular:

- ☐ one is that the audit committee is responsible for the relationship with the external auditor. This has the potential for conflict with the finance director and possibly the CEO but this should be manageable

- ☐ the report included sensible competence and independence tests and asserts that one member of the committee needs to have recent, relevant financial experience. However, it could be argued that if one person is nominated as an 'expert', this could potentially single them out for special attention in the event of litigation

- ☐ the report proposed a few new rules such as that the company chairman should not be an audit committee member, and that there is a need for disclosure if there is no internal audit function. It is worth adding to this that where an organisation has US obligations the audit and risk committee needs to also take into account the provision of Sarbanes Oxley

the way forward

The first thing an effective audit and risk committee will do is to clarify its scope and objectives. These must be seen alongside all other matters reserved for the board and any other adjacent committee such as health and safety.

Part of this process will be to determine its structure and workings, including membership, frequency of meetings, administrative support and its interfacing with key players including the board. Setting the agenda for each meeting is too important to be left to the secretary or the executive. It should be the responsibility of the chairman, who needs to consult widely.

Its second key task is to create the right climate within the organisation. This is a core responsibility of the chair of the audit committee. He or she must encourage openness and build relationships with the company chair, the CEO, the finance director, internal audit and the business heads.

An open, frank relationship with the external audit team is also an imperative. This requires an investment of time. The committee needs to ensure the resources are appropriate to give the assurances needed. The chair must create a climate that encourages questioning and critical comments, while ensuring that this does not become destructive and unhelpful.

Its third area of focus is to identify the important issues. What are the 'right issues' that will give the assurance or lead to value addition? This should include a review of the accounts, accounting policies, risk management and controls. Keeping an eye on the quality of earnings and complex transactions is also important.

external auditors

The external auditors must be up to the job. They need to have a team that possesses the right skills and chemistry to work effectively with the various stakeholders in their zone. They need to be independent and seen to be independent. They need to be able to demonstrate a clear understanding of the industry and the company. Above all, they too must add value as well as provide assurance.

The audit committee has the responsibility to see that value for money is achieved and that the cost/value equation is positive. Areas for closer inspection include:

☐ whether the auditors work in partnership with internal audit

☐ whether the plans of both internal and external audit are optimised to avoid overlap and 'underlap?'

☐ how comprehensive and appropriate their audit plan is

common sense and trust

Audit and risk committees can and must add value. They will do this through hard work and diligence, using common sense and building trust with other key players – not through the application of complex rules and defensive sign-offs. As Warren Buffet has said: "Forget formulae and rules, common sense and trust are the most important factors in building value."

SAS, the leader in business intelligence software, asks...

Why get robbed of hard-earned profits when fraud is so easy to prevent?

OPERATIONAL EFFECTIVENESS

FRAUD PREVENTION

REGULATORY COMPLIANCE

RISK MANAGEMENT

CUSTOMER INTELLIGENCE

Fraud costs businesses €600,000,000,000 a year. SAS® software helps make sure it doesn't zero in on yours. We're the world's leader in business intelligence and analytics for financial services. SAS makes it easier to monitor every transaction for suspicious behaviour and stop every type of fraud in its tracks: credit card, identity, merchant, Internet transaction, brokerage and more. Analyse data to identify new fraud patterns. Constantly refine your alert engines. And track each fraud case through to reporting. To learn more about SAS visit our Web site or contact us on info.uk@suk.sas.com

www.sas.com/fsfraud

The Power to Know. | §sas.

investing for governance

Active investors are playing an increasingly important role in governance. Business ethics lecturer and author Alan Malachowski explains what such investors do and suggests how companies should respond

A swirl of confusion surrounds the role of so called 'active investors' in matters of governance. Who are they? What do they do? What are the economic and legal consequences of their actions? How do they differ from their 'passive' counterparts? Do they serve a useful function?

Some of the turmoil is caused by the ambiguity of the very phrase 'active investor', since it has two distinct interpretations within the business community. In the technical and more traditional sense, the phrase refers to the still seductive belief that the fate of investment income can be determined by 'managing' portfolio contents.

The idea that such control is possible is criticised by financial theorists, who claim that the efficiency of markets renders it redundant, if not absurd. The upshot of this powerful criticism is crisply summarised by William F. Sharpe, Nobel Laureate in Economics: "Properly measured, the average actively managed dollar must underperform the average passively managed dollar, net of costs. Empirical analyses that appear to contradict this principle are guilty of improper measurement".

EXECUTIVE SUMMARY

- ☐ the meaning of 'active investor' needs to be clarified

- ☐ 'active investors' should not be confused with 'activists'

- ☐ there are strong arguments against investor interference in matters of governance

- ☐ directors must be pro-active in responding to the phenomenon of active investing

On its second, wider and more topical interpretation, the term 'active investor' covers the various uses of investments, especially shares along with their accompanying voting rights, to influence the structure and behaviour of companies. It is in this sense that 'active investing' has become closely associated with the term of 'corporate governance'.

But, here too, there are troublesome ambiguities. To avoid them, we need to further distinguish between 'active' and 'activist' investors, a division that wisely separates the conservative approach of institutional investors from that of more radically inclined individuals and pressure groups.

institutional investors

Institutional investors are 'passive' in the traditional sense. The sheer size of their holdings prevents quick sales of underperforming stocks so they usually index their portfolios to broad market measures. But, they are active when it comes to the task of 'influencing the structure and behaviour of companies'. Not being able to move as swiftly within the market as individual investors, they sit back and try to improve its overall functioning.

Institutional investors do not form a monolithic group. They include pension funds, mutual funds, trusts and endowments. These can manifest significant differences regarding: investment objectives, fiduciary duties, attitudes to risk and assessment of good business practices. Nevertheless, when institutional investors take an 'active' approach to investment that encroaches on matters of governance they do so collectively.

Since they all manage assets on behalf of other parties, institutional investors want markets to perform well, and to do so as consistently as possible over the longer term. If they notice the kind of problems in relevant companies that threaten to prevent such an outcome, they will tend to intervene to attempt to resolve those problems. Thus, for example, in the UK, institutional investors have put a lot of pressure on companies to bring their remuneration policies back into line with economic performance in the light of huge perceived discrepancies in this regard. And more specifically, in the US, pension plans recently forced the Disney Corporation to separate the positions of chief executive and chairman.

how active should institutional investors be?

Those who have the power to do something they believe to be in their own interests will sooner or later go ahead and do it (and probably sooner rather than later). So, it is not surprising that powerful institutional investors, who can form even more powerful alliances when it suits them, have become 'economic interventionists'. However, it remains to be seen whether they are engaging companies at the right level.

Some argue that such 'institutions' ought to foreswear the 'can do/will do' principle of power, and thus refrain from meddling in the affairs of companies about which they are unlikely to have the necessary knowledge and expertise. They should, instead, work towards the inculcation of very general principles of good governance without taking the reins out of executives' hands.

Others object even to this. They want institutional investors to facilitate 'market solutions' to problems of governance simply by allocating funds in ways that reward the most efficient uses of resources and correspondingly punish those that are inefficient, thereby letting 'good practice' rise to its own natural level in its own time and in its own way. This kind of argument is pressed particularly hard by those who fear that with the advent of funds that are 'screened' for socially-damaging factors, institutional investors are starting to cross the line that divides them from 'activists'.

the growth of activism

Whether to intervene or not has become an issue for investors partly as a result of historical developments. In the US, for example, the question could not even arise in most cases until regulations that protected management's right to manage entirely by its own lights were revoked from the 1950s onwards. This happened when the Security and Exchange Commission and the courts began not just to endorse but enforce the view that companies are run for the benefit of stockholders rather than managers.

This seemingly innocuous view opened the floodgates for shareholder pro-posals of a social and political nature and, hence, for 'activism' as we now know it. For the view implied that a hard-nosed stance such as that taken by Greyhound in 1946, when it excluded a resolution to abolish racially segregated seating on buses on the grounds of its irrelevance to the proper concerns of its business, was no longer tenable. Shareholders began to have the final say on the nature of such concerns. Today's activists in the 'socially responsible investment' movement tend to forget that their current push towards 'progressivism' in business had these historical precedents.

how should the board respond?

This lapse of memory highlights an inherent weakness in investor activism: because it invariably follows fashions in 'socio-political opinion', it lacks staying power. That does not mean companies should keep their heads down until such activism goes away. Good directors will always factor the possible responses of both active and activist investors into their risk assessment strategies.

When institutional investors show the first signs of dissatisfaction with particular processes of governance, directors need to see this as a wake up call. Their primary task is then to consider whether the correlative changes in policy make good business sense. If they do not, then they should be proactive in taking the argument to that effect to the investors themselves without special pleading, and well before the momentum of opinion goes against them.

Virtually the same goes for activists and their various socio-political agendas. These may often seem ephemeral, but they can still pack a punch that damages the value of a business, not to mention the careers of its managers. Directors must develop skills in assessing the consequences of activist proposals, especially over the longer term. They should then develop governance policies accordingly, and prepare to defend them in public forums.

Good governance requires, above all, a steady hand on the tiller and a sharp eye on commercial objectives when the waves of investor activism rise up in the business community.

CHAPTER 8

CSR: the first steps

Sir Adrian Cadbury, chairman of the committee that produced the seminal 1992 report on corporate governance, offers advice for companies that want to develop policies on social responsibility

Corporate social responsibility (CSR) is now an accepted part of good governance. The first page of the Combined Code includes the supporting principle that: "The board should set the company's values and standards and ensure that its obligations to its shareholders *and others* are understood and met."

In July 2000, the 1995 Pensions Act was amended to include the requirement that pension funds disclose in their Statement of Investment Principles, "the extent (if at all) to which social, environmental and ethical considerations are taken into account in the selection, retention and realisation of investments."

This change prompted the Association of British Insurers to tell its members: "Public interest in corporate social responsibility has grown to the point where it seems helpful for institutional shareholders to set out basic disclosure principles, which will guide them in seeking to engage with companies in which they invest." This is an encouragement to investors to raise social, environmental and ethical issues with companies in which they hold shares.

the general business case

But CSR is not an issue just for listed companies, or those whose global network of interests exposes them to increased social and environmental risks. It is relevant for virtually all established businesses.

EXECUTIVE SUMMARY

- ☐ corporate social responsibility is increasingly important to investors, employees and customers
- ☐ to succeed, CSR initiatives need commitment at board level
- ☐ public pressure is not, of itself, a reason to adopt a cause: you must believe in what you do
- ☐ reporting on CSR should focus on descriptions of the activities undertaken and the progress being made

A monthly consumer survey carried out in the UK asks the question: "How important is the social responsibility of a business to you when you are purchasing a product?" In 1998, 28 per cent answered 'very important'; by 2001, that figure had grown to 46 per cent.

Society's expectations of business are rising. And this has implications beyond the customer base. Those companies that are seen to be successfully combining commercial aims with social ones will have the edge in recruitment. Many of the most able and thoughtful people are looking to join companies with a reputation both for enterprise and for social responsibility. They want to work for businesses that are respected.

The arguments for CSR, therefore, have as much to do with business sustainability as morality.

practical steps

What, then, are the areas where companies and the community meet, and where commercial and social aims can be combined? They can be grouped under three main headings: education, community activities, resource saving and the environment.

☐ education

There are innumerable ways for companies to interact with the educational world. Links with schools or colleges can include serving on governing bodies or committees, helping pupils who have difficulties with reading or maths, providing equipment (or helping make the most of equipment already in place), giving practical assistance in vocational or business studies, or offering projects or work experience.

The first steps are to find out what the needs of local schools and colleges are and match them with what you have to offer. Very often, business/education partnerships involve the commitment of people and time rather than money. It is important to find out what the team with whom you work care most about and where they would most like to make a difference. You will need to know what relevant experience and skills they have.

You can also, of course, help the community through in-house 'education'. The far-sighted business invests in training that goes beyond the specifics of the 'job-in-hand'. It may, for example, offer the workforce opportunities to acquire computer or IT skills, or help staff from ethnic minorities to learn English. It recognises that improving the local skills base will improve the local economy – to the benefit of all.

☐ community activities

Companies need to be good 'neighbours'. This means thinking about the effects on the community of noise, emissions, inconsiderately parked vehicles, untidy refuse and so on.

They also need to make positive, direct contributions. This means assisting with local projects, helping to make play areas for schools, planting trees and landscaping derelict areas, coaching local teams, supporting particular appeals for good causes and generally giving their backing to voluntary activities going on in the community.

Perhaps one of the most helpful contributions companies can make is to invest in projects to improve the local economic environment. I chair a body called the Aston Reinvestment Trust (ART) that lends to businesses and social enterprises in disadvantaged areas and the inner city. Loans are given where applicants have been turned down by a bank, where there is an acceptable business plan and where there is the prospect of a 'social return'. The return in the case of small businesses is usually safeguarding or creating jobs. We have so far lent to 200 enterprises and protected or created around 1,000 jobs.

☐ resource saving and the environment

Office equipment manufacturer Ricoh provides a good example of what can be achieved in the field of resource saving. Its aim is zero waste, finding a profitable use for everything that comes into the plant. The scheme started with modest targets for reprocessing, recycling and re-selling anything that was not part of the company's final output. Such is the enthusiasm of its workforce for the project that it is now hitting a figure of 95 per cent usage of inputs.

Many companies have simple schemes for measuring their use of resources such as electricity and water, or logging the cost of waste disposal. These schemes concentrate attention on how these costs arise – which in itself identifies opportunities for savings.

Improved management of resources benefits both businesses and society and can be highly motivating to people working on a site. It is easy to inspire a spirit of competitiveness between departments or sites in order to achieve continuous improvement.

In the wider environmental arena, companies should reduce pollution, curb CO_2 emissions and, where possible, use renewable resources.

the principles

For CSR projects to succeed, certain "rules" and guidelines should be borne in mind. Some of the main ones are given below.

☐ **believe in what you do**

What you undertake must accord with the values you share with your workforce. Do not become involved in the social field purely because of external pressures. And do not allow CSR to distract you from business-critical issues. Your primary corporate responsibility to society is to deliver needed goods and services and to do so profitably. Get that right before setting 'wider' social goals.

☐ **go with the grain of the company**

Entries into the social field should harness the energy and enthusiasm of the working team. Tap the ideas of your team and back causes in which they are already voluntarily engaged. Well-chosen social involvement can be a powerful motivational tool. Think of the satisfaction that comes from helping to build a school in India. Or even, at a more prosaic level, of winning an inter-departmental competition to save energy.

CSR IN THE WORKPLACE: RELATING TO EMPLOYEES

When SAS opened for business in 1976, it had five employees and founders with a vision of the ideal workplace. Today, it is the largest privately owned software company in the world, with revenues of $1.34bn and more than 9,300 employees worldwide

SAS's workplace has always reflected the founders' vision of an environment that nurtures creativity, innovation and quality in which employees both thrive and excel. The culture embodies the basic SAS philosophy: if you treat employees as if they make a difference to the company, they will make a difference to the company. At the heart of this business model is a simple idea: satisfied employees create satisfied customers.

The company's culture is based on trust between employees and the company. It rewards innovation, encourages employees to try new things, but does not penalise them for taking chances. It is a culture that cares about employees' personal and professional growth. SAS employees work in an environment that fosters and encourages the integration of the company's business objectives with their personal needs. Employee benefits are designed to remove distractions, save employees time, and to make their lives outside work less stressful. As a result, employee turnover has never been greater than five per cent and is consistently below the industry average of 20 per cent. And SAS's employee-friendly programmes pay for themselves. According to Professor Jeffrey Pfeffer at Stanford University's Graduate School of Business, who has made a study of the company, SAS's low staff turnover saves the company between $60-80m a year in recruiting and training costs alone. In addition, in nearly 30 years of business, SAS has always been profitable and never laid off a single employee.

SAS's work environment continues to receive awards. In the US, it has been ranked among *Fortune* magazine's list of 100 Best Places to Work for seven consecutive years, most recently ranking number eight. Many of SAS's European offices, including the UK office, have achieved good rankings in similar surveys in the last few years. In addition, the company's business model is regularly used in case studies by universities such as Stanford, MIT Sloan School of Management, and Wharton.

☐ show commitment

Commitment by a company to whatever they undertake outside their normal run of business is crucial. And it must come from the top. As is written in Corinthians, "For if the trumpet give an uncertain sound, who shall prepare himself to the battle?" It is the certainty of your call to action that will determine the success of the undertaking. Without commitment and clarity of purpose, initiatives can degenerate into token gestures.

THE IMPORTANCE OF ETHICS

According to a survey conducted by research group Echo, most members of the financial community see a strong link between the concepts of corporate social responsibility, business ethics and corporate governance. The survey was based on analysis of press and media reports, and interviews with decision makers in the UK, USA, France, Germany, South Africa and Australia.

"Business ethics are where most businesses start to look at particular issues relating to corporate governance and social and environmental matters," said a senior executive of the FTSE Group. "If you think of Enron as an example, it was a complete corporate governance failure; a failure brought about by a total lack of business ethics by individuals in the organisation creating what was effectively a fraudulent act. And that comes back to a challenge: what are business ethics and the principles of business?"

This view was echoed by one of the South African interviewees: "Governance, ethics and CSR are closely interlinked. The core of corporate governance is business ethics," argued the compliance director of a leading investment service. "They are all linked to the moral fibre of our business. You can't be cheating on one and trying to do good on the others. There is a correlation and a congruence between these three," said the HR head of a securities bank.

In Germany, there was a view that the three parts would interlock more tightly over time. "You have to understand CSR as part of corporate governance. At the moment, that might not be the subject of the discussion, but that is where it is going to be. CSR and corporate governance are going to grow closely together."

However, others detected differences. One UK interviewee remarked that: "Business ethics is pure and broad. CSR and corporate governance are more focused. At the extreme, no-one buys shares due to all these issues – but for normal companies, it's a blurred link." Another said: "Corporate governance is different – more about meeting internal legal requirements. CSR is not like that – it's about how a company deals with its consumers."

Some respondents believed the three concepts were independent. "There is no connection. You can act ethically without having to become a social benefactor. You can do business in the normal way without having to go deeper into social sponsoring." The US title Business Report commented: "Enron's corporate governance statement was enough to make your eyes weep, but look what happened to it".

The survey found much greater unanimity as regards the rationale for, and benefits of, having a corporate code of ethics. A large majority believed that "a code of ethics is useful for corporate reputation", but were adamant that such a code is not mainly for PR. And most agreed that: "not having a code is an increasing negative for institutional shareholders."

☐ measure and report on CSR effectively

You need to know how well your purpose is being achieved; measure therefore what is relevant to that end. Report on social activities by describing them, rather than by trying to present them on an artificial financial basis. Many of the activities described above do not lend themselves to being treated in accounting terms. Reports should reflect what you need to know to manage these activities and what your workforce wants to know for their satisfaction.

Some areas of social responsibility – such as waste management – are income-earning. Others, such as school partnerships or in-company training have costs, but also bring benefits. The links with schools may assist an individual company's recruitment and will advantage business more generally in terms of raising educational standards and presenting an accurate and positive picture of careers in industry and commerce. In-house training contributes to productivity and to the community's skill base.

Costs and benefits have to be balanced, and striking that balance is a matter for each company to decide for itself.

GETTING INVOLVED: USEFUL CONTACTS

Business in the Community
Exists to "support business in continually improving its impact on society". Works with schools and runs enterprise programmes in deprived areas. **www.bitc.org.uk**

National Education Business Partnership Network
An umbrella organisation for 138 education business partnerships throughout the UK. www.nebpn.org

Young Enterprise
Runs enterprise-education projects in schools with support from local and national businesses. www.young-enterprise.org.uk

Prince's Trust
Charity working for disadvantaged 14 to 30-year olds. Last year, helped 4,359 young people start their own businesses. www.princes-trust.org.uk

National Federation of Enterprise Agencies
Independent not-for-profit network of local enterprise agencies that help small and growing businesses survives. Works with schools to promote the idea that working for yourself is a viable career option. **www.nfea.com**

SAS, the leader in business intelligence software, challenges...

Achieve corporate compliance now.
Or watch investor confidence shatter.

ENTERPRISE INTELLIGENCE

SUPPLIER INTELLIGENCE

ORGANISATIONAL INTELLIGENCE

CUSTOMER INTELLIGENCE

INTELLIGENCE PLATFORM

SAS® Corporate Compliance software provides a complete infrastructure to inventory, monitor, audit and authenticate your disclosure controls and procedures. So you can achieve compliance with regulations while protecting your reputation and shareholder value. SAS enables you to deliver accurate, timely financial statements that minimise operational risk. Prepare now for any new regulations. And focus your time on managing your business. To learn more about SAS visit our Web site or contact us on info.uk@suk.sas.com

www.sas.com/compliance

The Power to Know.

building a better board

Devoting time and energy to the selection, structuring and developing of the board will help ensure that it and its individual directors are up to the job, says Chris Pierce, corporate governance author

The purpose of the board is to ensure the organisation's prosperity by directing the organisation's affairs while meeting the appropriate interests of its shareholders and relevant stakeholders.

If the board is to be effective its members must be properly selected, organised and led.

board composition and organisation

To maximise board potential, the chairman can consider a number of strategies:

☐ increase the number of executive and non-executive directors (NEDs)

☐ make more use of external resources within the board's networks and of any under-exploited resources

☐ increase the capability of the board in areas of strategic thinking

☐ develop the knowledge and expertise of existing directors

☐ develop the board by looking at processes in use.

EXECUTIVE SUMMARY

☐ due care should be given to board selection and succession

☐ board members' skills, expertise and experience should complement one another

☐ the performance of individual directors needs regular monitoring and ongoing development

☐ once the structure is right, the board must work through a series of further developmental stages

In the following action lists you will see a number of tasks that will help lead to improvements in the board's membership and methods. These tasks should be undertaken with like-minded colleagues from the board. Many of the issues may cause conflict, especially where directors have lost touch with current methods and thinking.

ACTION LIST

☐ review the ratio and number of executive and non executive directors

☐ consider the energy, experience, knowledge, skills and personal attributes of current and prospective directors in relation to the future needs of the board as a whole, and develop specifications and processes for new appointments as necessary

☐ identify potential candidates for the board, make selection and agree terms of appointment, and remuneration, with all new appointments being agreed by every board member

☐ provide new board members with a comprehensive induction to the board

☐ monitor and appraise rigorously and regularly each individual's performance, behaviour, knowledge, effectiveness and values

☐ identify development needs and training opportunities for existing and potential directors and the company secretary

---

roles and responsibilities of the board

Having reviewed the board's composition, a chairman is then in a strong position to look at the board's workings. Does it try to do too much itself? In what ways could its corporate direction processes be more effectively handled?

ACTION LIST

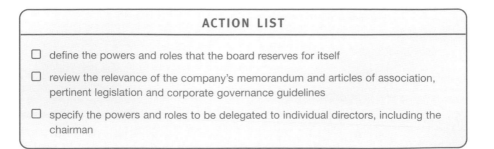

☐ define the powers and roles that the board reserves for itself

☐ review the relevance of the company's memorandum and articles of association, pertinent legislation and corporate governance guidelines

☐ specify the powers and roles to be delegated to individual directors, including the chairman

ACTION LIST

- ☐ specify the powers to be delegated to board committees and determine their terms of reference, life span, leadership and membership

- ☐ empower the managing director to implement the decisions of the board and other specific matters not reserved to the board itself, and confirm such empowerment by a formal resolution to the board

board and committee meetings

At this stage, the board should review its procedures. Even the smallest of family-run businesses will benefit from regularisation of what may be a lunchtime chat. This is especially true if the time for succession to the top posts is approaching.

ACTION LIST

- ☐ establish, maintain and develop reporting and meeting procedures for the board and its committees

- ☐ determine policy for the frequency, purpose, conduct and duration of the meetings, and especially the setting of the agenda

- ☐ create a comprehensive agenda covering all the necessary and appropriate issues through the year while also including important immediate issues

- ☐ assign tasks and objectives to individual members, including especially the chairman, managing director, finance director and company secretary, and agree the working relationships between them

- ☐ define and review regularly the information needs of the board

- ☐ adopt efficient and timely methods for informing and briefing board members prior to meetings

- ☐ maintain proper focus on the board's key roles and tasks, ensuring that major strategic issues affecting the company's visibility, reputation and prosperity are addressed

- ☐ allow sufficient time for important matters to be discussed thoroughly

- ☐ encourage all directors to attend all board meetings and to contribute

- ☐ ensure that adequate board minutes are kept and that attendance and decisions are properly recorded

developing the effective board

Board development should be seen as an integral part of the normal work of the board. It should be owned and managed by the board as a whole. The chairman of the board is likely to play a leading and co-ordinating role.

mapping development needs

A diagnostic framework should include the following:

- ☐ knowledge, skills and understanding
- ☐ directors' qualities and attributes
- ☐ the board as a working group, including decision making processes

what to do

There are a number of activities that can be introduced to the board as part of its development strategy.

analysis of current performance

All members should be asked to look through the documentation of the past few meetings of their board and answer the following questions:

- ☐ to what extent has the board focused on the key directorial issues?
- ☐ how does the board monitor its performance?

discussions

Development can occur through discussions at board meetings. However, boards may address this issue more effectively by adopting separate structures such as board forums, working parties or task forces.

mentors

Some long-established members of the board may accept the responsibility of acting as mentors to new members. The role may include inducting them to the

THE TYSON REPORT

Following the 2003 review by Derek Higgs into the role and effectiveness of independent non-executive directors, professor Laura Tyson, dean of the London Business School, was asked to lead a drive to broaden the pool of potential candidates available to join major company boards. Here she summarises her task force's report:

The Report on the Recruitment and Development of Non-Executive Directors, published in June 2003, suggests that many UK companies would benefit from widening their search for non-executive directors (NEDs) and adopting rigorous and transparent procedures for recruitment. The report suggests that possible sources of talented candidates that traditional, largely informal, search processes have tended to overlook include: the so-called 'marzipan layer' of corporate management just below board level management; unlisted companies and private equity firms; business services firms and consultancies; and organisations in the non-commercial sector.

The report says that the business case for diversity can be made on both the benefit of wider perspectives and the benefit to company reputation. Not only does diversity in the backgrounds, skills and experiences of NEDs enhance board effectiveness by bringing a wider range of perspectives and knowledge to bear on issues of company performance, strategy and risk, but board diversity can also send a positive and motivating signal to customers, shareholders and employees.

The task force decided against drawing up a list of 100 potential NED candidates from the non-commercial sector as suggested in the Higgs review. The report concludes that it would have been "a disservice to both companies and talented individuals to propose such a list without rigorous and transparent search and without reference to the particular situations and challenges of companies seeking to identify such candidates."

However, it did recommend the establishment of an annual census to measure diversity on the boards of UK publicly-listed companies and encourage progress in this area. The report maintains that such measurement is an important driver for change in how companies recruit, retain and reward talent. It is anticipated that the census would become part of a high-visibility initiative that would also disseminate best-practice examples of how individual companies build more meritocratic and diverse boards and foster research on the business benefits of greater board diversity.

board, initiating them into the way the board works and encouraging regular discussion and review of the new member's development.

On the other hand, some members may prefer to have a director of another, non-competitive organisation undertake this role, since there is the possibility of personal conflict arising from the board's normal activities.

away days

One way to improve directors' understanding of each other's strengths, experiences and background is to get everyone to spend time together off-site in a more relaxed environment. Away from the day-to-day pressures and interruptions of office life, the focus of sharp minds can develop the strategic business plan or mission statement, or reappraise company goals in a far shorter time.

use of consultants

Many companies find that an experienced developer is an effective catalyst for improving the cohesiveness of the whole board. He or she may sit in on board meetings, acting as a constructive critic to the board as a whole, and/or offering individual directors development and guidance as necessary. The chairman may also benefit from the guidance of a suitably qualified and experienced consultant by, say, working together to restructure board meetings and agenda items.

There are boards whose directors work so closely together in the day-to-day management of the business that they find difficulty in standing back and considering policy and longer-term strategic issues. This situation applies particularly to smaller companies whose directors often have a significant shareholding and a functional management responsibility.

individual performance review

Every board member's learning must be linked to performance objectives. These objectives should set out the actions that will lead to a significant improvement in performance. Performance reviews need to be held regularly and cover both the business performance and progress towards making agreed changes.

introducing board development into an organisation

In order to maximise the benefits of board development, you should consider taking the introductory process through a number of stages:

☐ **obtaining buy-in from the chairman and managing director**
The developer has to form a working relationship with the board and especially the chairman and managing director. Support from the top

signals to others in the company that development is an important activity within the organisation.

☐ **move to board responsibility for self development**
The next stage is to encourage the board to take responsibility for its own growth, as a continuous process. This must be a combination of individual director development and team improvement.

☐ **include/budget for board/director development in the business plan**
In any organisation there are influential people who can add weight to a strategy or programme and make all the difference to whether it happens or not. You know who they are in your own business. You need to make sure they are on side with the plan and are supportive.

☐ **identify the drivers and publish the plan internally**
Now it's time to tell the employees how their board is planning its developmental strategy and to make clear which individuals are responsible for driving the process. Support from the top needs to be stated openly and communicated in any company newsletters, notices, training programmes or videos.

☐ **agree route map and mark stages**
It's helpful to divide the plan into stages, each of which has its own actions, time plan and result. This allows checks on progress and helps to ensure that the plan doesn't lose direction. The stages should include the board as a whole and individual director development.

☐ **clear the roadblocks**
Many directors do not examine and question their assumptions. As a result they have a limited set of 'maps' setting their direction. They may erect elaborate defensive road blocks and create smoke screens that prevent themselves and anyone else from challenging either their actions or their assumptions.

The commonest roadblocks include:

☐ insufficiently compelling motivation in terms of beneficial outcomes

☐ lack of commitment from the chairman or other key gatekeepers

☐ insufficient budget

☐   time pressures

☐   unproductive competition between the directors

☐   rewards not linked to achievement of development objectives

You need to answer each of these blocks by:

☐   persuading the board of the benefits

☐   gaining commitment from other strong champions

☐   demonstrating the importance of having a board that is competent to lead the company into a profitable future

☐   accepting time pressures on directors, but showing that the board's priority should be the long-term health of the company

☐   highlighting the directors' duty to work together for the good of the company

☐   establishing a link between reward and development objectives

---

ACTION LIST

☐ set and achieve objectives for continuous improvement in the quality and effectiveness of board performance, including performance in a crisis

☐ review regularly the degree to which the board's objectives are achieved

☐ review regularly the quality of the board's decisions, advice and information received and consequent action taken

☐ consider the impact on board effectiveness of directors' attitudes to handling risks, failure, ethical issues, change, commitment and challenges to their interpersonal relationships and their decision-making styles

☐ identify and influence the strengths and weaknesses of individual directors where these affect the performance of the board as a whole

☐ take appropriate action, including the use of training and external specialists to maximise efficiency and the effectiveness of board work

technology issues

Professor Jim Norton, senior policy adviser on e-business and e-government at the IoD, looks at some of the board's main duties in managing ICT projects

"Nothing is more difficult than to introduce a new order. Because the innovator has for enemies all those who have done well under the old conditions and lukewarm defenders in those who may do well under the new."

Niccolo Machiavelli, The Prince, 1513.

the challenge

Nearly 500 years ago, Machiavelli understood well just how difficult it is to drive through change. Information and communications technology (ICT) can engender ambivalent feelings, as it is often the tool through which change is implemented.

We are bombarded, in both private and public sectors, with stories of ICT projects that have gone over time, over budget, or have simply failed. Perhaps the most widely respected regular survey of global ICT projects is that carried out by the Standish Group. Its latest data suggests that only 16 per cent of projects are brought in on time, on budget and to specification. Some 31 per cent are cancelled during implementation and the remaining 53 per cent suffer from budget over-run, late delivery, or reduced functionality – often all three. Boards should recognise that there is a clear

> ### EXECUTIVE SUMMARY
>
> ☐ the cost and importance of ICT projects make them a central risk-management issue
>
> ☐ effective systems improve business performance and aid the flow of information to and from the board
>
> ☐ successful implementations depend on investment in people as well as technologies and tools
>
> ☐ the responsible board ensures its network is secure and has contingency plans for system failure

TECHNOLOGY: THE BUSINESS PARTNER

Corporate governance should include a recognition that board directors need to have a full understanding of technology issues, says Brendon Kirby, IT director at Barclays Bank

In order to deliver on strategy, organisations need to use technology efficiently and effectively. However, this is easier said than done: many technology initiatives fail, either because the technology doesn't deliver what it claimed it could, or because it falls short of forecasted financial benefits.

The relationship that the technology part of the business has with its business areas, together with the perceived role of technology within the organisation, will dictate ultimately the value it can contribute to the overall success of the organisation.

Developing the right kind of relationship is critical. Partnering, where business and technical areas each mind their own area of expertise and responsibility while respecting the capability of the other, is the ideal. It is the only one where the capability of both technical and business areas can be fully leveraged.

Building a partnering culture requires capability in both technology and business areas. On the technology side, there needs to be an understanding of how technology can support business needs and a willingness to work closely with business people. On the business side, there needs to be an understanding of how the business works at a detailed level, as well as a readiness to work with technology people. In both areas, there must be a pool of people who hold the knowledge, capability and experience to deliver change effectively.

Establishing a partnering culture requires buy-in at the highest level. Distrust or a lack of understanding of technology at board level is often the reason for a poor relationship between business and technology areas. It is therefore important that board members have some understanding of technology as it applies to their organisation. However, it is more important that they understand not only what is being spent, but what it is being spent on. The only way this will happen is to develop a partnering relationship with technology.

correlation between the size of the project and the risk of failure. Projects budgeted at more than £10m are at particular risk.

Given this depressing backdrop, why should we press on with ICT investment? The answer lies in the immense power of well designed and well implemented ICT systems, embedded in good business processes, to make substantial improvements to business performance. Effective systems can address all of the key areas of interest to the board:

- [ ] cost reduction

- [ ] quality improvement

- [ ] customer reach and satisfaction

- [ ] more effective use of physical and knowledge assets

Decision making at all levels can be sharply improved by access to accurate, timely management information.

responding to the challenge

The key governance issue for boards is to recognise that ICT makes an excellent servant but a poor master. The purchase of ICT systems is generally only part of a wider programme of business change. Such change must be firmly grounded in the business plans of the organisation, with clear aims and measureable outcomes. The 'people' aspects, in terms of re-organisation, training, internal communications and motivation, must be properly planned and resourced.

Boards should ensure that management teams follow the guidelines below.

1. beware the status quo

Don't replicate in software and silicon the processes currently in use. Even the most junior of users will be delighted to tell you what is wrong and time-wasting in the current methods if you take the trouble to ask. A few users – those who understand the potential of new technology as well as the details of the tasks being carried out – will go further and give you real breakthroughs in process change.

2. budget honestly

If people are at least equal partners with ICT systems in delivering service, then they deserve to have at least half of the project budget allocated to them. Investment must be made in:

- [ ] communicating why change is required and how it will be achieved

- [ ] developing the new skills required

- [ ] rewarding positive change

3. provide genuine champions

People need role models they can relate to. Find the practitioners (managers, salespeople, marketing staff, finance team members, administrators, and so on) who already have experience of the real benefits that well designed new systems can bring; use them to evangelise change to a wider audience.

4. deal with disincentives

Recognise that the business and performance measurement models of existing units may need to be changed, as detail of the old models may contain big disincentives to the use of new processes and technology. For example, new systems may be critically dependent on staff accurately capturing data when stock is moved or sold, yet performance measurement systems might not recognise the time required to do this or monitor and reward accuracy.

5. challenge pay and conditions

Don't be frightened to overhaul existing structures of pay and conditions of service. Business change might need pay and bonus incentives in order to be driven through. Recognise that efficiency will initially fall rather than rise during the transition to new systems.

6. don't over centralise

A number of smaller linked systems may be more effective (and less vulnerable) than a single mega system.

security and continuity

Simply developing and implementing effective systems is not enough. It is imperative to ensure they operate reliably – even under difficult conditions. The board, as a key element of its implementation of the 'Turnbull' risk management requirements (see chapter 6), needs to ensure the holistic treatment of security issues. Physical, personnel and electronic security are all linked. As indicated in the annual information security breaches surveys carried out by PricewaterhouseCoopers for the Department of Trade and Industry, the biggest risk to the integrity of key ICT systems remains internal attack from a disaffected staff member rather than external hacking.

Too many companies focus on just one element of the security triangle. It is vital to ensure that all are addressed consistently. Too often, excellent electronic and physical security is undermined by poor internal processes.

The board should ensure that full business continuity plans are in place, with provision for alternative locations and protection of key staff and records. The starting point is to understand which of the organisation's ICT systems are 'mission critical' and then develop clear priorities for restoration from backup sites and systems. These plans must be regularly updated and tested.

Where networked communications and internet access are important for business operation, for example, in co-ordinating activities up and down the supply chain, the board should insist that management has credible plans for dealing with electronic attack. This can take many forms: at its simplest, the disruption caused by viruses from email attachments; at its most complex, direct 'hacking' attempts on key company servers or databases.

Perhaps the most insidious form is the so-called 'Distributed Denial of Service' (DDoS) attack. In such an attack, a company's systems are not directly penetrated: they are bombarded with false traffic from a myriad of sources so that the company's genuine traffic and transactions cannot get through. This is the cyber equivalent of a sit-down protest outside a high-street store. No damage is done to the store but no customers can get in and so no business can be transacted.

A very close working relationship is required with your company's telecommunications and information service providers to deal with such an attack, filtering out the rogue traffic before it can congest access to the company's systems.

a final thought

The motto for ICT mediated business change should be, in the words of American architect, inventor and philosopher Buckminster Fuller: "…rather than attempting to teach people the right things to do, one should design organisations such that doing the right things is simply the path of least resistance."

measuring performance

John Wilkes, head of performance management at SAS UK, and David McWilliam, senior consultant on corporate governance at the IoD, look at key elements in the boardroom self-evaluation process

Measurement is an established principle of good corporate governance. The Combined Code on Corporate Governance, appended to the listing rules of the London Stock Exchange, states: "The board should undertake a formal and rigorous annual evaluation of its own performance and that of its committees and individual directors".

EXECUTIVE SUMMARY

☐ corporate and board performance both need to be measured. Corporate measures should be:

– specific to the organisation and its competitive strategy

– seen in the context of historic and sectoral information

– used to promote discussion and decide actions

☐ boards need regularly to focus on specific measures of their own governance performance

☐ IT can help store and manage the information needed to assess both corporate and board performance

The very first principle of the Combined Code also clearly and logically links the performance of the board to that of the company, so that the ultimate measure must be how well the business has done. It states that: "Every company should be headed by an effective board, which is collectively responsible for the success of the company".

Good performance, which is maintained consistently, through difficult as well as comparatively easy times, taking sound advantage of periods of opportunity and defending the company successfully in the event of a crisis occurring, is the intended outcome of good governance.

what should you measure and how?

Although board and corporate performance are inextricably linked, it is important to measure each separately.

With regard to corporate performance, a study carried out by Cranfield Centre for Business Performance in December 2003, 'Corporate Performance Management', found that there were four fundamental characteristics of good performance measurement. They are:

- ☐ broad-based measures
- ☐ structured understanding of strategy
- ☐ feedback on performance
- ☐ action on results

Assessment should cover not only financial performance but also strategic development and 'softer', cultural issues. It follows that the board should have a clear understanding of its goals, its direction and its ethos; companies that know their businesses, know which levers to pull to improve performance.

Evaluation must be seen as a practical rather than an academic exercise. Results of performance measurement should be fed through to all relevant staff; targets for improvement should be set.

choosing key corporate performance indicators

Key corporate performance indicators (KPIs) should be company-specific and reflect the company's circumstances, stage of development and objectives.

Market share growth is a criterion when building a business; customer lifetime value is important when focusing on profitability and cost to serve. If a company wants to be known for excellent customer service, KPIs could include:

- ☐ time taken to deal with enquiries and complaints
- ☐ levels of customer satisfaction
- ☐ time taken to process and fulfil orders

Measures should be both quantitative and qualitative. If one of your goals is to improve human resources management you will need to look not only at statistics for staff turnover and absenteeism but also at feedback given in appraisal interviews.

The golden rule here is to make sure that there is a clear rationale for any measure used.

measuring the board and governance itself

The accumulation of factual evidence, from McKinsey's early research in 2000 to Deutsche Bank's current evaluation (see chapter 4), shows that corporate governance has a significant impact on risk, profitability and performance. Well-governed companies have consistently outperformed those with low standards.

McKinsey's further survey of global investor opinion in July 2002 showed that investors put corporate governance on a par with financial indicators when making investment decisions. Premiums paid for companies displaying good governance ranged from 12 per cent in North America and Western Europe to more than 30 per cent in Eastern Europe and Africa. 'Rigorous evaluation' must, therefore, include evaluation of the system of governance itself.

Investors in the McKinsey survey looked particularly for:

- ☐ timely, broad disclosure
- ☐ independent boards
- ☐ effective board practices and processes
- ☐ performance-related compensation

Companies need to know how they 'measure up' in each of these areas. Assessment should be more than a box-ticking exercise; it should take the form of careful, qualitative study. How committed are we to the principle of transparency? How much non-financial information do we include in our report and accounts? How independent are our non-executives? How effective are our long-term incentive plans for directors?

asking the hard questions

The board must ask itself some tough questions and be willing to give honest answers. It must assess corporate performance, board performance and the performance of individual directors, at both executive and non-executive levels.

Below are some key questions that might be used.

corporate results

☐   how has the company performed against previous years? (actual)

☐   how has it performed against the strategy and plan? (subjective)

☐   and against comparable businesses? (objective)

the board as a whole

☐   does it work as a team?

☐   is it leading and controlling the company?

☐   does it contribute valuably to the strategy?

☐   does it manage risks effectively?

☐   is it capable of reacting well to a crisis in a way that protects the company's reputation among investors and the public?

the individual directors

☐   are they part of the team?

☐   do they contribute to debate?

☐   are they prepared to question and challenge?

☐   can they commit the necessary time?

☐   is their knowledge and understanding of governance adequate and up-to-date?

More detailed suggestions for a boardroom questionnaire can be found in the box on page 83. The Combined Code also provides some good examples.

No one questionnaire, however, will be suitable for all. Each company will have its own particular board structure and style; each board will need to develop its own self-evaluation process. Companies will need to pick and choose from the examples given and add questions of their own.

To achieve objectivity, boards should consider using an independent facilitator: a third party might be able to see things that the team 'in-house' can't.

managing information

Accurate and fair assessment of the company's position depends on the flow of the right information to the board. Directors must be able to see current statistics and data in the context of historical and sectoral trends: few figures mean much in isolation; comparisons need to be made.

IT can be the mechanism to collect and store the right information. Information from the base transaction systems and external sources can be summarised and made consistent and then 'published' on a common IT platform for analysis and reporting.

Analytic and data mining software can be used to help identify trends, predict future performance, anticipate problems and draw conclusions.

using results

The outcomes should be: to enable the creation of key objectives for further board and business improvement; work towards the highest standards of governance and best practice; and create a succession plan that will match the company's strategy.

Whatever the method of evaluation, the board must have the integrity and courage to act on the results. In some circumstances, this may mean making changes to the executive and non-executive teams. The evaluation should not simply be based on current performance, but must meet the needs of the future, in the light of a changing world and evolving strategy.

A company is, ultimately, only as good as its board. Corporate performance and board performance are inextricably linked.

SAMPLE BOARD QUESTIONNAIRE

board meeting processes

- [ ] are we discussing the right issues at meetings?
- [ ] how can the processes be improved?
- [ ] is appropriate, timely information of the right length, format and quality provided to the board?
- [ ] do presentations tend to duplicate board papers? Should they be shorter?
- [ ] is there enough time for discussion and sufficient opportunity to raise issues of concern?
- [ ] should 'non-executives' item for discussion' be tabled on the agenda?
- [ ] are board meetings the right length?
- [ ] are the minutes too long?
- [ ] are the minutes helpful?
- [ ] does the number of board and committee meetings enable proper consideration of the issues?

composition of the board

- [ ] is the board balanced in terms of, for example, the number of non-executives and executives?
- [ ] does the board have the right mix of knowledge and skills?

other issues

- [ ] commercial skills – does the group have the necessary commercial skills in the operating business units?
- [ ] corporate social responsibility – has the company made real progress in CSR; is it doing enough; are its activities sufficiently visible?

Abridged from an Independent Director Briefing given at the IoD in February 2004 by Philip Bramwell, company secretary and general counsel of mobile communications group, mm02

future perfect

> **Mark Goyder, director of the business-led think tank Tomorrow's Company, looks at how corporate governance can best progress**

How do we picture a company? We used to think of it as a machine. Managers operated the controls. Directors, elected by and known to the shareholders, ensured that investors would receive a good return and that the company kept its nose clean. This was 'doing things by the book'.

There are some medium-sized enterprises, some venture-capital-financed companies and some family companies where this model still applies. But, in general, there is no book to do things by now.

EXECUTIVE SUMMARY

- ☐ the key to the board's role lies in tracking relationships, not following procedures
- ☐ boardroom sycophancy must end; new directors must feel able to say that the emperor has no clothes
- ☐ leaders must not be remote to the public and employees; they should get out and find out what is really going on
- ☐ there should be less cult of the CEO and the reward for failure should be to stick around, helping others learn from the past

the changing environment

Small companies have become more entrepreneurial and fast on their feet. Large ones have got larger still; and so have the rewards of those who manage them. The speed with which businesses must respond has accelerated.

The shape of companies has been changed by alliances, joint ventures and global operations. Directors' salaries are sometimes dwarfed by those of scarce and talented specialists.

Investment, too, has become more international; and diverse. A chunk of the shares may be owned by hedge funds, and when the AGM comes around some of those shares may be voted by intermediaries who have borrowed them purely for this purpose. (See 'Restoring Trust: investment in the twenty-first century', Tomorrow's Company, 2004.) Companies' licence to operate has also become more complicated, as they strive to avoid the opprobrium of increasingly influential NGOs, or live up to many international codes created by their peers. Business operations are conducted in a transparent global goldfish bowl, where one employee's error of judgment may create a ripple effect all around the world.

the emerging model

So how should we picture the company? Today, we are learning to think of it as a living organism, balanced delicately in a web of overlapping relationships, each of which has to be sensitively nurtured. Front-line employees are the antennae and carry the company's reputation; processes are the pulse; middle-management the blood. Leadership is the beating heart that energises that blood supply and makes it consistent. Governance is the central nervous system, operating key reflexes that avert danger, and pulling together all the communication from and to the outside world into a coherent whole.

At the head of the company of the future, leaders talk not of 'doing things by the manual' but of establishing a culture and a tradition that will inform the decisions and initiatives of front line staff without the need to refer to base.

Only the most retarded organisations will now limit themselves to thinking about governance as box-ticking and compliance.

the continuing flaws

Boardroom behaviour needs to adapt, and adapt fast. Too often, at present, the smart thing for the newly arrived director to do is to show they have read the papers and ask some question of detail about the numbers that have been prepared in a vast book that is put in front of them every month.

And then we wonder why it is that highly qualified directors miss major frauds and strategic errors. There is too much posturing; too much pretence that everyone knows everything. Too few boardrooms engender an atmosphere in which a director can say: "Hang on, this doesn't make sense."

This has implications for the board and especially the chairman. The board meeting of the future may well retain the disciplines of periodic reporting against budget, and regular risk management, but it is also going to have to be far more open to hearing the informal commonsense wisdom that lurks in the organisation. As a 2002 study by Tomorrow's Company, 'Lessons from Enron', revealed, the key question a new board member should be asking is: "never mind the well-polished reports. Are we equipped to find out what is really going on?"

the ideal model

Imagine a world in which companies felt able to admit mistakes and deal with failure as a fact of life. AGMs would be looked forward to as occasions when you could learn from the criticisms and suggestions of shareholders. Annual reports would faithfully track the ups and downs of the company on its long-term journey. On or near the front page there would be, among other things, a statement and accompanying graph showing the ratio between the lowest and highest paid person in the organisation, with accompanying commentary explaining changes in the distribution of awards.

A core of long-term owners of shares would regularly challenge the CEO about performance and progress towards the targets.

Instead of payments for failure, the likeliest punishment for a CEO who had made a mess of things would be to stay on for a year, helping to dig the company out of debt, working out the notice period, supporting the successor and passing on the most valuable lessons of all – those that come from past failure. There would be no pretence that the arrival of a new CEO heralded the beginning of history: continuity would be valued.

Companies would undertake surveys of their customers and then invite them to presentations at which they shared the feedback, good, bad and ugly, with employees and customers together. Long-term supplier relationships would be based on a foundation of trust, which started from a clear declaration of the way the two or more parties would do business with and behave towards each other.

Leaders would not be remote figures, hiding behind the tinted glass of their limousines, as they swept away from AGM bilious with impotent protest. For a week every year they would go out into the front line with service engineers or undertake a spell of community service.

Boards, too, would be accessible and self-critical groups. They would review their own performance and give their own CEO and chairman marks out of ten. The unscripted appearance of an independent director at one of the plant's premises to sit in on some meetings and take a bowl of canteen soup with a random group of employees would be unsurprising: when employees had serious doubts about the ethics of a new directive from on high, they would know that in extremis they could e-mail or phone a board member.

fact not fiction

Idealistic? Yes. A fantasy world far in the future? No, actually.

With only one exception, every example above is based on a real-life business involved with Tomorrow's Company.

Never mind about combined codes and institutional shareholders, committees and the ritual completion of remote questionnaires. This is the real heartland of better leadership and governance.

checklist for the board

Consider if high standards of corporate governance are integrated into your company's strategy;

Ensure your board is aware that the company's bottom line performance can be enhanced by good corporate governance;

Emphasise to your board that the price of a governance failure can be high;

Highlight the importance of a thorough process of risk management to the company's future security and profitability;

Ensure the board addresses the needs of key stakeholders in the company – including investors, employees, customers and the wider community?

Does the board itself need strengthening – or diversifying?

How is the board's performance – and corporate performance – being monitored effectively? Examine the measures used;

Examine the improved use of technology within the company to enhance board information and corporate performance measurement.

further information

Institute of Directors:	www.iod.com
SAS:	www.sas.com
Deutsche Bank:	www.db.com
McKinsey & Co:	www.mckinsey.com
Echo Research:	www.echoresearch.com
London Stock Exchange:	www.londonstockexchange.com
London Business School:	www.london.london.edu
Tomorrow's Company:	www.tomorrowscompany.com